Protecting Our Own

Perspectives on a Multiracial America series

Joe R. Feagin, Texas A&M University, series editor

The racial composition of the United States is rapidly changing. Books in the series will explore various aspects of the coming multiracial society, one in which European-Americans are no longer the majority and where issues of white-on-black racism have been joined by many other challenges to white dominance.

Titles:

Melanie Bush, *Breaking the Code of Good Intentions*

Amir Mavasti and Karyn McKinney, *Unwelcome Immigrants: Middle Eastern Lives in America*

Richard Rees, *Shades of Difference: A History of Ethnicity in America*

Katheryn Russell-Brown, *Protecting Our Own: Race, Crime, and African Americans*

Forthcoming titles include:

Erica Chito Childs, *Fade to Black and White*

Elizabeth M. Aranda, *Puerto Rican Hearts and Minds*

Protecting Our Own

Race, Crime, and African Americans

Katheryn Russell-Brown

ROWMAN & LITTLEFIELD PUBLISHERS, INC.
Lanham • Boulder • New York • Toronto • Oxford

ROWMAN & LITTLEFIELD PUBLISHERS, INC.
Published in the United States of America
by Rowman & Littlefield Publishers, Inc.
A wholly owned subsidary of The Rowman & Littlefield Publishers Group, Inc.
4501 Forbes Boulevard, Suite 200, Lanham, Maryland 20706
www.rowmanlittlefield.com

PO Box 317
Oxford
OX2 9RU, UK

British Library Cataloguing in Publication Information Available

Library of Congress Cataloging-in-Publication Data

Russell-Brown, Katheryn, 1961–
    Protecting our own : race, crime, and African Americans / Katheryn Russell-Brown.
        p. cm.
    Includes bibliographical references and index.
    ISBN-13: 978-0-7425-4570-0 (cloth : alk. paper)
    ISBN-10: 0-7425-4570-9 (cloth : alk. paper)
    ISBN-13: 978-0-7425-4571-7 (pbk. : alk. paper)
    ISBN-10: 0-7425-4571-7 (pbk. : alk. paper)
    1. Discrimination in criminal justice administration—United States.   2. Crime and
    race—United States.   3. African American criminals.   4. Racism—United States.
    5. African Americans—Psychology.   6. African Americans—Race identity.   7. Group
    identity—United States.   I. Title.   HV9950.R8727   2006
    364.3'496073—dc22

                                                                        2005022464

Printed in the United States of America

⊚ ™ The paper used in this publication meets the minimum requirements of American
National Standard for Information Sciences—Permanence of Paper for Printed Library
Materials, ANSI/NISO Z39.48-1992.

To my husband, Kevin
and our beautiful children, Louis and Sasha

CONTENTS

FOREWORD

A row of young Black girls are sitting on a bench in a playground waiting their turn to play a game. One of them, Edna Mae, is jumping up and down, giggling at everything and generally acting silly. A teenager watching the group yells at her, "Edna Mae. Act your age and not your color."

The admonishment is a classic stereotype, rendered worse because it was unleashed by one Black youth against another. In fact, Edna Mae, at age seven, *is* acting her age. But the teenager views her antics as somehow an unhappy attribute of her race. As the incident reveals, such racial associations are deep, afflicting persons of all races, and are very difficult to uncover, much less erase.

Regrettably, the admonishment, "act your age and not your color," might be an appropriate reminder to those Blacks who substitute color for common sense in choosing to defend Blacks who neither need nor particularly merit our concern. Why do we rise up to defend O.J., a womanizer of White women, and not get group mad about the systematic job bias against Blacks under seemingly neutral racial policies that have a devastating impact on Black employment? Katheryn Russell-Brown examines and critiques this illogical and unproductive phenomenon that she calls "Black protectionism."

She understands as we all understand the history, both ancient and contemporary, that motivates Black peoples' distrust of a White-oriented structural system. The more than two centuries of slavery in the United States, as awful as they were, might have been consigned to history had they not been followed by economic arrangements designed to continue the exploitation and subordination of Black people. Control was maintained by systematic policies of intimidation and violence, including four thousand known lynchings and perhaps as many deaths during massacres, misnamed "riots"—in places as geographically diverse as Colfax, Louisiana; New York City; Tulsa, Oklahoma; Rosewood, Florida; and Elaine, Arkansas.

Blatant racial segregation has given way to a multitude of discriminatory practices that over time have eroded much of the civil-rights era gains. As Professor Russell-Brown points out, the gaps between Blacks and Whites in every area of well-being—education, income, wealth, employment, housing, and health care—are large and growing larger. It is not necessary to deny that many Blacks are doing well compared to their parents and grandparents, but the progress of some of us tends to obscure how poverty, AIDS, family dysfunction, and police harassment serve to hold most Blacks in a racially marginal and vulnerable condition.

These facts are real, but the influences of the media, including the careful manipulation of racial news, results in Blacks not receiving information that they really need to know. This lack of knowledge, not much corrected by even publications and television programming aimed at Black listeners, leads to a distortion of militance. We focus on the high living and often outrageous foibles of Black celebrities. There is close to an obsession over whether or not Michael Jackson molests young boys to the exclusion of concern over the fates of thousands of young Black males who, according to statistics, will spend much of their lives in prison.

As a people identified by skin color, we remain society's scapegoats. The fact that so many Whites seek to assuage the growing unease about their status and well-being, are willing to view their troubles as the result of court decisions sanctioning abortion and same-sex marriage, does not insulate us from group attack if the political and economic problems can in that way be resolved or—more likely—sidetracked.

With this as background, much more fully developed by Professor Russell-Brown, we can perceive if not justify the support the Black community offers some high-profile Blacks and not others, including those far more deserving of our defense. Why do so many of us rally behind O.J. Simpson and Michael Jackson, or cheer for Tiger Woods, when these individuals don't want to even identify with Blacks and, because of their wealth and fame, don't have to identify?

Along with a number of Black law teachers, I urged Blacks to look at Clarence Thomas's civil rights record before supporting his nomination to the U.S. Supreme Court. Our warnings were ignored by the clamor to "give the brother a chance." Well, almost fifteen years later, Thomas's record on the Court has been one of close identification with the most conservative ideologies. He regularly votes against Black interests in affirmative action, voting rights, the death penalty, jury discrimination, and due process in criminal cases. Actually, the list of Justice Thomas's judicial betrayals to the Blacks who supported him is long. The harm he has done in the law and to the lives of Black people—and will continue to do—is discouraging in the extreme.

And yet our traditional civil rights organizations appear mesmerized by Blacks who gain powerful positions. To cite just one painful example, both the NAACP and the Urban League have given awards and recognition to Secretary of State Condoleezza Rice rather obviously because she is Black, and despite her advocacy of the Iraq War that is proving a disaster to this country in ways too painful to enumerate. Secretary Rice doesn't need or deserve recognition when the political party she represents favors policies clearly detrimental to Black people.

In comparison, neither our civil rights organizations or Blacks in general offered much support to Professor Lani Guinier or to Dr. Joycelyn Elders when then-president Bill Clinton pulled the rug out from under both of them to avoid political problems he feared might result from the truths about electoral apportionment policies that Professor Guinier, his appointee as assistant attorney general for civil rights, had written; and the discussion of masturbation in sex education courses that Dr. Elders, his surgeon general, suggested was appropriate. Clinton treated both women shabbily with, evidently, little concern about public criticism from Blacks, of which there was very little.

As Professor Russell-Brown suggests, the silence may have been due to what I call the unholy alliance of Blacks with Bill Clinton. Here, as with so many politicians, it was a matter of embracing style while ignoring substance. We focused on his many appointments of Black federal judges and other high-level officials and pretended not to notice how little real support he provided to programs that Blacks needed. He urged that we "end welfare as we know it," a phrase that placed the emphasis on unwed, Black mothers who cheated on welfare. He didn't say that, but he didn't have to.

The image of Blacks as welfare cheats was deeply set. The real welfare, of course, goes to the corporations and defense contractors who, unless their misdeeds shock the conscience, are not criticized and seldom successfully prosecuted.

I recognize that we often rise to defend Blacks like former D.C. Mayor Marion Barry or Jesse Jackson who have broken laws or ethical standards when we see that the government or the public is "piling on," treating well-known Blacks more harshly than Whites in similar predicaments. Even here, we tend to overreact, as we did in staunchly defending Bill Clinton who faced impeachment for lying about his sexual encounters with a White House intern, Monica Lewinsky. I confess that I was among those who rose in his defense, less to condone his conduct than to prevent Republicans from using that conduct to force him from the presidency.

Black people were not alone in defending Clinton. A great many Whites joined us in turning back the politically motivated impeachment action. We won that battle, but as the two presidential elections that followed have shown, at too high a price. Some of the Blacks Professor Russell-Brown interviewed maintain that we "must defend our own." Fair enough, once we determine who deserves both the designation and the protection that our support can provide.

Derrick Bell
Visiting Professor of Law
New York University

ACKNOWLEDGMENTS

Thanks to Joe Feagin for his interest in this project. When I first discussed the book idea with him he was quick to suggest that it would be a great fit with a series he was editing at Rowman & Littlefield—Perspectives on a Multiracial America. The press's editor, Alan McClare, was equally enthusiastic about the project and has always looked for ways to answer yes to my many questions. And a heartfelt thank you to Derrick Bell for allowing himself to be nudged into writing the foreword.

My new academic home, the University of Florida, College of Law, has been wonderfully supportive of this project. Dean Robert Jerry and Associate Dean Patrick Shannon made funds available to conduct the focus groups discussed in this book. A special nod to my colleagues Kenneth Nunn and Sharon Rush, who offered incisive remarks and questions about Black protectionism.

I greatly benefited from working with several people, including Amanda Moras, a graduate student in sociology at the University of Florida. She worked tirelessly on the focus groups, met with me weekly over a four-month period, and read through several versions of the chapters and always managed, somehow, to offer fresh and thoughtful suggestions. As always, my former graduate student, Melissa Bamba (who is now the assistant director of UF's Center for the Study of Race and Race Relations) made detailed and critical comments, chapter-by-chapter. Jeffri-Anne Wilder helped organize two of the focus groups.

ACKNOWLEDGMENTS

Although I am unable to name them individually, I am greatly indebted to the thirty Gainesville, Florida, community members, working people, and students, who participated in the focus groups. This book is so much richer because of their insights.

A special thank you to the Department of Sociology at Northern Illinois University. Following my invited lecture in spring 2004, the audience plied me with provocative and important questions about the workings of Black protectionism. Likewise, comments I received from my presentation at the Second National People of Color and the Law Conference helped to shape the direction of this book. As well, Professor Randolph Stone offered a timely and spot-on evaluation of the manuscript.

There has been a lengthy gestation period for this book. I began thinking about these issues in 1995, during the O.J. Simpson criminal trial. Some of my earlier writings on the subject include a chapter in *Underground Codes: Race, Crime, and Related Fires* (New York University Press, 2004) and a law review article, "Black Protectionism as a Civil Rights Strategy" (*Buffalo Law Review*, 2005).

Finally, thank you Kevin for being my partner, every day. Thank you mom, for being my first and longest fan and for reading the manuscript cover-to-cover, in a few days. Thank you dad for showing me the joys of the writing life. The three of them, my husband and parents, over the course of dozens of conversations, helped me work through and construct the conceptual framework for Black protectionism.

INTRODUCTION

Despite my dad's best efforts, I still don't know a lot about blues music. I'm an R&B girl. One thing I do know, however, is that blues music can trick you because while the songs are classically "She/He/Somebody done me wrong" ones, they are often sung in such a way and accompanied by music that is so upbeat and so vibrant that you have to listen closely to the lyrics to know that the story is a sad, tortured one. The blues developed amid despair and glimmers of hope. Because blues music emerged from slavery, the music was political from the beginning. The blues are about Black people—our lives, hopes, and dreams. The blues are also about "the man," about racism, discrimination, and oppression—about the shackles of race. Blues music tells the story of a people trying to make sense of nonsensical and inhumane conditions. Of a people convinced that tomorrow promises to be better than today.

One blues song that captures the pain of racial oppression is the Razaf/Waller/Brooks classic, "(What Did I Do to Be So) Black and Blue?" The 1929 song, popularized by Louis Armstrong, concludes:

> Just 'cause you're black, folks think you lack,
> They laugh at you and scorn you too,
> What did I do to be so black and blue?
> When you are near they laugh and sneer,
> Set you aside and you're denied,
> What did I do to be so black and blue?
> How sad I am, each day I feel worse,

> My mark of Ham seems to be a curse!
> How will it end? Ain't got no friend,
> My only sin is in my skin.
> What did I do to be so black and blue?

The song puts into words the burdens of racial oppression. It captures the feeling of being part of a group that's been sentenced to second-tier status. Billie Holiday's "Strange Fruit" stands as a companion composition to "Black and Blue." Her song paints a harrowing word portrait of southern lynchings. While "Black and Blue" describes the personal pains of racism, "Strange Fruit" challenges us to act. Essentially it says, now that we know the truth of racism, we must *do* something. It begs us to consider what actions we can take to move forward.

Together, "Black and Blue" and "Strange Fruit" set the stage for understanding the protective response many African Americans have toward Black politicians and celebrities who find themselves in legal trouble. They "protect their own." Blacks protect their own because they believe no one else will; because they "remember when" Black men were strung from trees and lynched for being Black; because they believe Black people are still under siege; because they believe that if you're one of the lucky ones who's able to achieve some fame and fortune, you deserve a break; and because they truly believe that if Black folks are not vigilant and careful, they might find themselves back where they were one hundred years ago.

"Protecting our own" is nothing new. However, because there are increasingly more Blacks who have achieved mainstream success, the practice has newfound implications and consequences. Protecting our own, which I refer to as "Black protectionism," describes this phenomenon. It is the focal point of this book.

The O.J. Simpson criminal case sparked my interest in this topic. Simpson's trial is the best modern-day example of Black protectionism in action. In my first book, *The Color of Crime*, I raised and briefly discussed the issue of Black protectionism. My goal was to explain the Black community's collective embrace of Simpson. I was still intrigued by the topic, so for my second book, *Underground Codes*, I devoted an entire chapter to Black protectionism. Although the chapter and a subsequent law review article I wrote represented more than had been previously written on the topic, it was still incomplete. There was still so much more to think about, so many more questions to ask and answer, and a good deal more information to gather about the workings of Black protectionism.

In 2006, more than ten years following the Simpson acquittal, the case is still with us. Remarkably, O.J. Simpson is the poster child for the one who got away with murder. For many he is a symbol of the injustices of the criminal justice system. This is an interesting and troubling configuration—How is it that Simpson represents justice gone wild when so many others, before and after him, have robbed, raped, murdered, and pillaged millions without paying the piper? At the same time, why does O.J. Simpson stand as a cultural symbol of Black triumph over White oppression for so many African Americans? Why were so many African Americans so invested in the Simpson case?

Protecting Our Own considers these issues in detail. The book sets out to accomplish three goals. First, it attempts to define Black protectionism. This includes making the case that protectionism, as practiced by African Americans, is a unique and historically rooted phenomenon. Second, the book sets out to explain how Black protectionism works. This is done through a detailed examination of dozens of cases involving well-known Blacks who have faced accusations of criminal and ethical wrongdoing. And, third, the book considers how Black protectionism could be reformulated to work in the best interests of the African American community.

Chapter 1, "Loving O.J.: An Overview," lays the groundwork for a discussion of Black protectionism. Beyond defining Black protectionism, the discussion focuses on how Blacks fare in today's society. This offers a contemporary backdrop for understanding the strong love that African Americans show for high-profile members of the community who get in trouble with the law. The chapter also looks at the historical role of the Black athlete as a racial representative. The Simpson case provides a thread linking the old with the newer cases of Black protectionism.

In chapter 2, "Deep Roots and Long Branches," there is a historical and theoretical examination of the roots of Black protectionism. This includes an overview of the history of Blacks in the United States and the ways that the legal system, political system, and the social sciences joined to create and preserve Black oppression.

Chapter 3, "Clarence Thomas, O.J. Simpson, Jesse Jackson, and R. Kelly: Strange Bedfellows," considers the range of cases that have been eligible for Black protectionism. Between 1994 and 2004, there were more than thirty-four potential recipients of protectionism. These cases are divided into several categories. There is a discussion of cases involving politicians, those involving sexual assault, those involving Black women, and those involving athletes and rappers. The analysis offers an in-depth look at these high-profile cases, including how, whether, and why protectionism was granted.

Chapter 4, "Talking Community," incorporates voices from the African American community. The chapter reports the results of three focus groups conducted with a total of thirty local community members. Their keen insights raise important questions not only about how Black protectionism works, but how it *should* work. The participants strongly advocate expanding the reach of protectionism to include "the little guy"— the common Black person.

Chapter 5, "The Good, the Bad, and the Ugly" of Black protectionism, offers a detailed critique of Black protectionism. The chapter outlines the strengths and many weaknesses of protectionism as it currently operates. The discussion makes clear that significant changes need to be made in order for Black protectionism to fulfill its initial promise. For example, the need to expand protectionism to Black women, the need to hold Black celebrities accountable for their misdeeds, and the need to consider how, whether, and when the community benefits from protecting fallen celebrities.

Chapter 6, "Critical Black Protectionism," takes the best features of Black protectionism and reworks them to make the practice an effective and reliable tool to promote racial justice. In its new form, critical Black protectionism is no longer a knee-jerk response but rather a reflective and selective one. It requires more than Black skin to trigger the full weight and support of the Black community. Critical Black protectionism focuses on whether applying protectionism in particular cases benefits the community at large, not just a few members.

Chapter 7, "Concluding Thoughts, New Directions," addresses additional questions and issues associated with Black protectionism. This includes a look at whether Black protectionism should extend to non-Blacks; whether others in addition to Blacks should be encouraged to engage in the practice; and the role of Black leadership in reframing the use of protectionism to support the Black community at large.

Blues music offers an apt metaphor for protectionism. Black protectionism is a kind of blues expression, a lyric, a voice that sings when called to action. In its best form, Black protectionism is a blues song of the Black community—a song that says remember your history, pay attention to the present, and continue to fight to ensure racial justice in the future.

© Bettmann/Corbis

"LOVING O.J.":
AN OVERVIEW

Introduction

"Aren't things better today than they were fifty years ago?" This is a common rhetorical query posed by those who have grown weary of race talk—weary of hearing that the fight for racial justice is still necessary. For those posing the question it is assumed that the only answer is "Yes."

Media representations of Blackness have indeed changed over the past fifty years. Images of African Americans in various mass mediums—including television, movies, newspapers, and magazines—are no longer confined to one-dimensional, negative stereotypes.[1] In previous decades, the portrayals were limited and predictable—the happy, hymn-singing, hired help; the sexual predator; or the tap-dancing entertainer.[2] Woefully absent were representations of Blacks as equal members of society—carrying their weight as citizens and gainfully and legally participating in their communities as workers, parents, and consumers.

Contemporary media images of African Americans are much broader and more complex. Today what is most striking is the visibility of African Americans. Blacks are depicted as having varied lots in life. They are portrayed as blue-, white-, and pink-collar workers;[3] they are shown as entertainers, professionals, politicians, and athletes; they are cast as friends, neighbors, coworkers, and confidantes; and they are depicted as society's dregs—drug addicts, scofflaws, and hardened criminals.

Although present-day portrayals of Blackness are more diverse than they were in the past, the most salient ones are representations at the

1

extremes. Mostly Blacks are shown as either the embodiment of the American dream or the embodiment of American failure—as symbols of hypersuccess or hyperdeviance.[4] In one corner there is Oprah Winfrey, Bill Cosby, Michael Jordan, Colin Powell, and Tiger Woods. They are often viewed as having transcended their race or as being colorless. In the other corner looms the Black slacker or criminal. He is either on the local news, as the Black man who robbed a store, or making national headlines, as the dangerous and hunted Black man (e.g., Washington, D.C. sniper, John Muhammad). All told, the media picture of the average, noncelebrity Black person is largely one of marginality and deviance—*the criminal blackman.*[5]

This chapter provides an overview of the issues associated with Black protectionism. This includes a definition of Black protectionism; how African Americans fare in today's society, when compared with Whites; the African American community's responses to high-profile cases involving African Americans, including the O.J. Simpson criminal trial; and why Black protectionism matters.

Defining Black Protectionism

"Black protectionism" describes the phenomenon of "protecting our own." It is what happens when the African American community rallies around its fallen heroes—those prominent Blacks who have been accused of wrongdoing. Although Blacks are not the only group that protects its own, Black protectionism is distinct in that it refers to the particular brand of assistance that the Black community provides for its celebrity members who face legal and ethical challenges. Black protectionism is defined as:

> The response by large numbers of the Black community to allegations that a famous Black person has engaged in a criminal act or ethical violation. The response is protective in that it denies, excuses, or minimizes the charges.

The historical basis for this practice and the specifics of how it operates are discussed in greater detail (see chapters 2 and 3). Now, with a working definition of protectionism, the next sections consider some of the issues raised by the term.

Is There a "Black Community"?

The concept of Black protectionism is based on three assumptions. First, that there is an identifiable Black community. This group includes Blacks in the United States—a number that minimally includes the more than 36 million African Americans who selected "Black" or "African American" as their race on the 2000 Census. This is a low-end number given that many African Americans (and Whites) adopt the "one-drop rule." According to this slavery-era practice, any person with "one-drop" of Black blood is considered Black. Thus, even Blacks who do not label themselves as "Black," or who label themselves as biracial or multiracial, may benefit from Black protectionism. O.J. Simpson is an example of the former and Tiger Woods an example of the latter. Woods, whose father is African American and whose mother is from Thailand, offers an interesting example of the long arm of Black protectionism. It is likely that if Woods found himself facing criminal charges he would receive support from the Black community. The application of the one-drop rule makes it difficult for someone to "opt-out" of Blackness—either by claiming colorlessness or allegiance to another racial group.

The second assumption of Black protectionism is that members of the African American community share a set of beliefs, perceptions, experiences, and history. Research shows that Blacks have distinct social views and beliefs based on life events. These include common perspectives on the group's access to education, health care, housing, and employment. Race-based viewpoints are notably acute regarding the criminal justice system. For instance, Blacks are much more likely than Whites to view the police and court systems as biased against Blacks. In particular, Blacks are more likely to believe that the police engage in racial profiling and are more likely to report that they or someone they know has been subject to racial profiling.

Given that Blacks in the United States represent the African diaspora, there is no single historical narrative that defines the group. However, Blacks living in the United States share a history of colonialism and oppression. Further, there is the experience of being "Black" in America— a tie that binds. This has resulted in the development of a specific American Black racial identification. Depending on their country of origin, Black immigrants to the United States arrive with a particular cultural background. Many, however, have noted that they have encountered the same racial bias and discrimination experienced by American-born Blacks.

As a result, many adopt a similar view regarding the presence of racial discrimination in the United States. It is important to note that many Blacks believe that they have a linked fate with other African Americans—that what happens to other Blacks in this country affects their lives.[6] This view is important to note because it helps to explain why Black protectionism is a popular practice. It sheds light on how a Black celebrity—a person who is far removed from the life and challenges of the average Black person— is viewed and treated as a representative for the Black community.

The third assumption, which is tied to the second one, is that group members have a way of expressing themselves communally—in such a manner that consensus, when it exists, can be measured. As indicated, polls and surveys that look at racial trends provide some insights into race-based perceptions and beliefs. Anecdotal and qualitative data support the idea that Blacks share a common set of beliefs, experiences, and perceptions. (For further discussion on the Black community's views on race, crime, and justice, see chapter 4.)

For the purposes of analyzing and discussing Black protectionism, I believe there is an identifiable Black community whose beliefs, viewpoints, and shared history can be examined. There is, however, legitimate debate about whether there is a cohesive Black community. It is clear as well that "race," therefore Blackness, is a social construction. Without question, the African American community is not a racial monolith. For example, the community has diverse views on education (e.g., public schools and vouchers), affirmative action, and which political party, if any, best represents the interests of African Americans. The problems inherent in treating the Black community as a monolith are discussed later in the book (see chapter 5).

Even though African Americans do not constitute a racial bloc, it is clear that in certain instances the community has a group-based response to public incidents involving high-profile African Americans. The community's response is distinct and identifiable, in part because its reaction is different from how other groups respond to the same incident. For instance, the polls indicating that 70 percent of Blacks (compared with 30 percent of Whites) supported Simpson are an indication of a group-based response to the charges. Likewise, the fact that more than two-thirds of all Blacks supported Clarence Thomas's nomination to the high court (compared with 52 percent of Whites) suggests there was a race-based view of the Thomas confirmation hearings.

Do Other Groups "Protect Their Own"?

This book clearly demonstrates that Blacks not only engage in protectionism, but that they engage in a type of protectionism that is unique to their history, experience, and conditions in the United States. That said, Blacks are not the only group that protects its own. The desire to protect and shield members of one's own group from recrimination and scorn is universal. Not surprisingly, other groups of color support and defend their members.

For instance, in the aftermath of the acquittals of the four officers in the Rodney King beating, some Korean American shopkeepers saw that their businesses were vulnerable to looting by African Americans. In response, some shopkeepers armed themselves with weapons to prevent theft. Some members of the Korean American community defended these actions; some argued that the shopkeepers were rightfully protecting their property and were being unfairly maligned. Some were critical, accusing the storeowners of harsh and violent attacks on Blacks. Many also observed that the mainstream press was fueling tensions between African Americans and Koreans.[7]

One example of ethnic protectionism was the response of the Cuban community to the Elian Gonzalez international custody case. The case, which took place in 2000, involved Gonzalez, a six-year-old Cuban boy. Elian arrived in the United States sans parents when his mother and others died in an ill-fated boat escape from Cuba. After being given temporary custody, Elian's Miami relatives were ordered to turn the boy over to the U.S. government. Their refusals led to a tense and costly household invasion by federal agents to retrieve Elian and return him to his father. Most notably, Miami Cubans were vocally supportive of the family's refusal to allow young Elian to be returned to his father in Cuba. For months, hundreds of people in Miami held vigils and thousands of people marched and demanded that Elian be allowed to stay in the United States.

It is not only people of color who practice protectionism; Whites also engage in the practice. The White responses to the acquittals in both the Rodney King and Amadou Diallo cases provide examples. Both cases involved charges of police brutality and in both instances the White officers were exonerated. In response to the charges, many Whites observed that the police have a tough job, that law enforcement officers have to make split-second judgments that should not be questioned, and that in the case of Rodney King, we do not know what happened (e.g., what King did before the video recording began). In sum, mistakes happen. White protectionism surfaced in the form of silence, following the acquittals in the King and Diallo cases. When the Diallo officers were acquitted, there was little talk by Whites of justice run amok. The White reaction in these cases varies greatly from the responses by the Black community. Following the not-guilty verdict for the officers involved in the Rodney King beating, there was widespread unrest and revolt in Black sections of Los Angeles. In New York, following the Diallo officers' acquittals, there were protest marches throughout the Black community.

The Martha Stewart case offers a different example. In the aftermath of the conviction of the home-design maven, White women in particular spoke out and criticized her criminal prosecution, conviction, and prison sentence.[8] Specifically, they questioned the treatment Stewart received, concluding it was harsh when compared with the treatment White men have received (those who have been accused of corporate criminality). Examples include male executives implicated in the Enron and World-Com corporate accounting scandals.

The above instances are offered as examples of White protectionism. Arguably, however, White protectionism is much more prevalent than the Diallo, King, or Stewart incidents indicate. A case can be made that for Whites protectionism is not limited to embracing and defending "fallen" White celebrities. Rather, the criminal justice system as an entity—one run by Whites—acts to protect those in power. Given this, as a group White Americans do not have to act as Black Americans do to protect their own—the justice system does it for them. Protection from the criminal justice system means that famous Whites are less likely to be accused or charged with criminal offenses and are less likely to be convicted of criminal offenses. Not only are Whites not as likely to be victims of racial profiling and police assaults, in a variety of ways they are shielded from the harshness of the justice system. Their charges are much more likely to be reduced, dismissed, or placed beyond the reach of the legal system. In this way the status quo is upheld. White privilege protects Whites from entering the justice system in the first place. It, therefore, diminishes their need to engage in the type of protectionism practiced by African Americans.

In addition to racial groups, some professions are known to protect their own. This includes police officers, medical doctors, and lawyers. The practice of police protecting their own is commonly referred to as "the blue wall of silence,"[9] while for doctors and lawyers it is known as closing ranks.

Black Protectionism as a Response to Racial Injustice

Black racial protectionism can be viewed as an attempt by members of the African American community to promote racial justice. The practice of "protecting our own" is a way of pointing out flaws within the justice system and reminding America that reforms are overdue. Race matters in the operation of the justice system. In this view, Black protectionism is one of numerous individual and community responses to racial injustice. These responses fall along a continuum that includes participating in rallies, giving speeches, engaging in boycotts, practicing jury nullification, voting in elections, filing lawsuits, writing letters to the editor, and publishing articles and books. Black protectionism is motivated by the same conditions that produce acts of civil disobedience, civil unrest, and other actions designed to trigger a sea change in racial politics.

Black Life—Just the Facts

Media representations aside, in real life African Americans are experiencing the best of times and the worst of times. At the same time that one-third of Blacks qualify as middle class, one-fourth live in poverty.[10] At the same time that 15 percent of Blacks attend college,[11] 32 percent of all young Black men are either in prison, in jail, on probation, or on parole.[12] Further, less than 50 percent of African Americans own their own homes.[13] Signs of racism, such as the number of lawsuits alleging discrimination in housing, employment, education, and politics (e.g., disenfranchisement), remain disproportionately high for African Americans.

The degree of Black racial progress, then, is a matter of interpretation. By many indicators, Blacks are doing better than they were fifty years ago. By many other measures, however, Black Americans are not doing well at all, especially when compared with White Americans. Some statistics in Black and White:

- In 2003, the Centers for Disease Control reported that 68.2 percent of Black children are born to unmarried mothers. This compares with 28.5 percent of White children.[14]

7

- According to the 2000 Census Bureau, 32.5 percent of Black households are headed by a single parent, while 11 percent of White households are headed by a single parent.[15]

- Eighteen percent of all Black children are born to teenagers. The figure is 10 percent for White children.[16]

- Between 2000 and 2001, 39 percent of the people on welfare were African American and 30 percent were White.[17]

- In 2000, the Department of Education reported that 13.1 percent of Blacks between the ages of 16 and 24 dropped out of high school. The figure is 7 percent for Whites.[18]

- March 2002 figures show that 11 percent of Blacks were unemployed, compared with 5 percent of Whites.[19]

- In 2001, the median per capita income for Blacks was $14,953, while the median income for Whites was $24,127.[20]

- The Black-White gap grows considerably when we compare wealth (e.g., property ownership, stocks, and bonds). In 2004, the median net worth of White households was $88,651 and $5,988 for Black households—a ratio of 15:1.[21]

- In 2003, the Centers for Disease Control found that 42 percent of the people living with AIDS are Black. The figure is 36 percent for Whites.[22]

- Blacks, who are 12 percent of the U.S. population, comprise 36 percent of the people in prison, on probation, and on parole.[23]

Some earlier figures provide a basis for comparison. For example, in 1959, almost 2 percent of all Whites were illiterate, compared with 7.5 percent of the non-White population.[24] In 1945, 28,280 Whites were in state or federal prisons, compared with 12,165 Blacks.[25] Accordingly, Blacks, who comprised nearly 10 percent of the U.S. population in 1945, were 30 percent of the prison population. In 1948, the median wage salary for Whites was $2,323, compared with $1,210 for non-Whites.[26]

The clear picture that emerges from these figures, old and new, is that there has been and continues to be a sizeable gap between Blacks and Whites on social indicators of success. These statistics force the question of whether it is even possible to bridge the racial gap between Blacks and Whites. The present-day conditions of African Americans did not fall out of the sky. They are directly connected to the group's history of enslavement in this country.[27] As detailed in the next chapter, this history includes centuries-long denials of the most basic human, civil, and property rights.

So, then, how do we answer the not-so-simple question posed at the beginning of the chapter—"Aren't things better today than they were 50 years ago"? To answer the question we have to take into consideration the lived experiences of African Americans—not just the surreal living circumstances of an elite group of visible African Americans. Armed with contemporary and historical facts about the Black experience in the United States, it would be folly *not* to question the degree of Black racial progress. Not surprisingly, many African Americans are acutely and intimately aware of this ugly history and its impact on their living and working conditions. This reality is brought to bear when African Americans evaluate social issues. In determining how African Americans respond to criminal charges against high-profile community members, this history carries a decisive weight.

Despite the fact that mainstream society often treats successful and well-known Blacks as exceptions, the African American community fully embraces them as one of its own. In fact, the community goes to great lengths to claim its high-profile members—even those who are ambivalent about their Blackness (e.g., O.J. Simpson) or those who identify as multiracial or biracial (e.g., Tiger Woods).

It is no surprise, then, that the African American community bestows a unique status upon those who have attained the American dream of riches and celebrity. The community accords them special treatment since they have succeeded despite the odds. African American success stories are closely watched and guarded.[28] Those who have managed to obtain large-scale prosperity, in spite of legal, political, economic, educational, and social barriers, are given the status of racial pioneers. It is, therefore, predictable that Blacks as a group are suspicious when criminal charges are brought against members of its elite, protected class. The Black community offers a wide net to its celebrity members who fall from grace: It protects its own.

This brings us to O.J. Simpson, whose criminal case catapulted the phenomenon of Black protectionism onto the national stage. The Simpson case serves as a classic representation of the workings of protectionism.

O.J.: The Spectacle

The O.J. Simpson criminal case left little to wish for. It had all the elements of a top-rated, prime-time television drama—race, sex, class, celebrity, violence, a handsome defendant, attractive victims, unpredictable witnesses, stoic jurors, dueling attorneys, and Hollywood! From the low-speed car chase to the acquittal, the Simpson case produced a long series of jaw droppers. It also brought us never-before-seen images of how race, class, gender, fame, and crime can intersect and collide in a court case.

The very public handling of the case broke new ground on many fronts. In addition to catapulting Court-TV, the Simpson trial demonstrated the public's fascination with all things celebrity. Americans, en masse, not only videotaped and watched the trial on television, they also watched the ever-growing number of shows devoted to "analyzing O.J." Dozens of books, published prior to, during, and after the Simpson trial, became best-sellers. For ever more details, insights, and tidbits—on the case and the courtroom players—the public looked to the newspapers and tabloids. And, ten years after the acquittal, the nation and media's O.J. fever is hard to forget. It was obsession, it was fascination, it was all O.J. all the time.

Although Americans in the North, South, East, and West were riveted by the case, we tuned in with different perspectives and for different reasons. In fact, the persistent rent in the thread of the nation's interest was race. Over the course of the eighteen-month case, polls consistently trumpeted the Black-White divide. Surveys reported that 70 percent of African Americans staunchly supported Simpson's claims of innocence. At the same time, 70 percent of Whites believed that Simpson was guilty of murdering his ex-wife Nicole Simpson and her friend, Ronald Goldman. Given that Whites and Blacks brought starkly different perspectives to the case, it is not surprising that Whites and Blacks interpreted the court proceedings through distinctly different racial lenses.

The Verdict

On October 3, 1995, at 10:00 a.m. Pacific Standard Time, 95 million people turned on their televisions and radios to hear the verdict in *California v. Simpson*. I, too, watched as the Los Angeles County court clerk read the verdict, "We the jury, in the above titled action, find the defendant, Orenthal James Simpson not guilty of the crime of murder." For seconds, maybe a minute, I stood staring at the small, black and white television I kept in my office. As a student of U.S. racial history, I had been certain that O.J., even with all his money and fame, would be convicted. He was, after all, still Black.

My surprise at the verdict, however, was nothing compared with my surprise at the postverdict reactions. Two things startled and unsettled me. First, the way that many African Americans reacted to the acquittal. Split television screens and newspaper photographs showed some Blacks joyously celebrating the jury's decision. We saw Black people, men and women, old and young, in business suits and sweat suits, jumping up and down, high-fiving each other, proclaiming that, finally, justice had been done. For me, the Black community's reaction to the verdict was an unexpected replay of its response to the U.S. Supreme Court's decision in *Brown v. Board of Education*, in which the Court outlawed racial segregation in public education.

On the other side of the split screen, White shock quickly turned to steam-blowing anger. Whites were fuming mad. This was the second thing that unsettled me about the Simpson verdict—the White reaction to the Black reaction to the case. White anger about the case outcome was not just something on television. It was visible in the real world—at work, on the streets, at the mall, and on T-shirts. Whites everywhere were mad: It was more than just a few, random Whites, in one area of the country, of one economic class, of one political party. Whites were very upset—and not just those who were members of racist hate groups, such as the Ku Klux Klan.

Certainly history provides images of angry Whites, including lynch mobs and the Klan. However, I could not recall recent examples of White rage. During the 1960s civil rights struggles, we regularly saw photographs and file footage of large groups of self-righteous and demonstrably angry Whites—intransigent Whites who opposed granting Blacks civil rights. They hurled racist epithets at Blacks, they blocked school entrances to

Black children who had been granted the legal right to enroll and attend, they refused to serve Black restaurant patrons, they forced dogs on Black men, women, and children, and they sprayed water hoses on Blacks who demanded racial justice.

The White reaction to the Simpson acquittal was White anger *deja vu*. And, much like the anti-integration Whites, those Whites shown on the other side of the split-screen were angry and appeared to be on the verge of serious violence if not restrained. The question remains, why were so many White folks so fighting mad? It is remarkable that the Simpson case, which on its face addressed neither social nor political issues, brought out such widespread investment in its outcome. As noted earlier, the White response to the not-guilty verdict is notable given their muted responses to other socially charged cases, such as the acquittals of the police officers in the Amadou Diallo and Rodney King cases.

While I was taken aback at the White responses, I was most intrigued and interested in exploring the Black community's responses. After the verdict, Black support for Simpson peaked at 82 percent. While some of this support may have been a response to pride in Simpson's Black defense attorney, Johnnie Cochran, strong Black community support for Simpson existed before the trial began and before Cochran took on the role of lead defense attorney. Why was the African American community so solidly behind Simpson? Was it tied to the White response to the case, the long history of racial oppression or individual African Americans' experiences with the criminal justice system? Was the answer one of these, all of the above, or were there other reasons?

The Athlete as a Race Representative

Thinking about Black reaction to the Simpson case means thinking about the overall role of Black athletes within the Black community. From early on, athletes have been among the first "credits to their race," the first to achieve outward markers of success, including large homes, fancy cars, and fine furs. As larger than life symbols of historically negative Black stereotypes—including the Black brute and the dumb jock—Black athletes have publicly carried the lion's share of the race weight. Black athletes have had to fight against the racist perception that they are physically and intellectually inferior to Whites (see chapter 2). The creation of the

Negro Leagues in baseball is just one example of how Black athletes were excluded from the mainstream. Successful Black jocks in basketball, football, baseball, and boxing have legendary status within the community. Their fight to be accepted as worthy and skilled competitors paralleled the larger struggle for Black racial justice.

Historically, athletic competitions involving Black sports figures have led to racial conflicts and violence. Perhaps the best known of these was the boxing matchup between Jack Johnson and Jim Jeffries, who was dubbed "the Great White Hope."[29] Jeffries had to be lured out of retirement to fight Johnson. Finally, the large purse and the push to defend the athletic superiority of the White race propelled him to return to the ring.

The title fight was held on July 4, 1910, in Las Vegas. There were thousands of people, mostly White men, in attendance. Throughout the fight, the crowd taunted Johnson with racial slurs. Johnson defeated Jeffries in a long and brutal fifteen-round match. Johnson had succeeded in becoming the first Black heavyweight champion. Johnson's win was cause for major celebration throughout the Black community, nationwide. His win was seen as public proof that Blacks could stand toe to toe with Whites in an athletic contest. For many Blacks, Johnson's win displayed the best his race had to offer.

Johnson, who boasted of his in-the-ring capabilities and was often seen in the company of White women, was loathed by many Whites. White anger was so intense following his victory that race riots erupted in cities across the country. More than two dozen people were killed, scores of people were seriously injured in the violent outbreaks, and the police made hundreds of arrests for disorderly conduct.[30] One official indication of the degree of White resentment was the swift passage of federal and local legislation that made it a crime to transport pictures of the fight across state lines.[31] Another was the barely masked anger in a *Los Angeles Times* editorial, "Word to the Black Man," published two days after Johnson's win:

> Do not point your nose too high. Do not swell your chest too much. Do not boast too loudly. Do not be puffed up. Let not your ambition be inordinate or take a wrong direction. Remember you have done nothing at all. You are just the same member of society you were last week. You are on no higher plane, deserve no new consideration and will get none.[32]

Johnson was later convicted of violating the Mann Act, a federal statute that prohibited taking women across state lines for prostitution. Although the conviction was later exposed as a sham, Johnson was sentenced to more than a year behind bars—which he served following his return to the United States years later.

Jack Johnson is one of many Black athletes who have had to carry the race mantle. For numerous other sports figures—e.g., Jesse Owens, Jackie Robinson, Elijah "Pumpsie" Green, Curtis Flood, Joe Louis, and Muhammad Ali—their athletic prowess served as a proxy for the humanity of the Black race.

O.J. Simpson, then, was one in a long line of Black athletes who stared down racism and beat the odds. Simpson, one of the first Black college football players to win the coveted Heisman trophy, was the first pick in the 1968 draft, a star halfback for the Buffalo Bills, an All-American, and was inducted into the NFL Hall of Fame. Simpson's stellar athletic career led to fame, riches, and mass popularity. For Blacks, he was living proof that the American dream was attainable. Simpson showed that Blacks could overcome centuries of entrenched racism to achieve mainstream success and wealth. He also represented the notion that some Blacks could "transcend" their race, become colorless in the eyes of Whites, and obtain a pass into the White world.

For good or ill, O.J. was a unique Black hero, not just a sports hero. Not only was he adored by African Americans, he was embraced by Whites as well. O.J. was ours *and* he was theirs. Given this background, it is no surprise that a large number within the Black community viewed the 1994 criminal charges against O.J. as an attack on the entire community. He was a member of the community and one of its bright, shining stars. Simpson's fight against the murder charges became a fight to preserve his manhood, his dignity—in essence, his Blackness. Simpson's battle, although it was in the courtroom and not on the gridiron, looked like other, earlier racial fights that Blacks had witnessed: a fight featuring a lone Black man fighting an unjust and racist criminal justice system.

In his battle against the notoriously corrupt LAPD, Simpson was positioned as "representing the race" in the same way Jack Johnson was in his fight against Jim Jeffries. Both the Simpson and Johnson "bouts" were viewed as fights against White oppression. Using this framework, O.J. begins to resemble Jesse Owens who won four gold medals in the 1936

Berlin Olympics—a solid debunking of Adolph Hitler's theories of a master race and Aryan superiority. O.J. looks like Joe Louis in his 1938 boxing match against Max Schmeling. And he takes on the appearance of Muhammad Ali in his fight to retain his heavyweight belt following his refusal to fight in the Vietnam War.

Throughout the entire Simpson episode there were questions about what the case actually represented. Was it about race, gender, class, celebrity, all of the above, or something else completely? It was clear that for many African Americans the Simpson case had quickly become a barometer of racial progress. For many, the role of race in Simpson's arrest, charge, and prosecution could not be denied. Although the case came to embody larger issues of race in American society, nagging questions remain. Did "loving O.J." move the Black community forward? Just how was it in our best interests to align ourselves with Simpson? As comedian Chris Rock asks in one of his routines about the Simpson case, "What . . . did we win?"[33] Should our collective embrace of Simpson and other Black celebrities be tempered by their perceptions of Blackness—by whether they take pride in being Black? Comments that Simpson made early in his career suggest that he took pride in being seen as "colorless":

> I was at a wedding, my [first] wife and a few friends were the only Negroes there, and I overheard a lady at the next table say, "Look, there's O.J. Simpson and some niggers." Isn't that weird? That sort of thing hurts me, even though it's what I strive for, to be a man first.[34]

All told, Black athletes have faced exclusion, scorn, ridicule, and racism. This background helped to make Simpson a sympathetic figure to many African Americans. The criminal charges in the Simpson case were more serious than those faced by Black athletes who preceded him. However, the racial taint of the criminal justice system made many Blacks question the charges, the crime, and the prosecution's overall case.

O.J. Becomes Emmett

While the Simpson verdict did not and indeed could not resolve large social issues, it did give us a picture of ourselves. It presented us with a carnival-mirror image—a distorted, uneven, and ultimately unflattering picture. Different people saw different pictures. Some saw a runaway criminal justice system; others saw a rich man's justice system at work; some saw a rich Black man who had been unfairly accused; still others saw the case as highlighting the perils faced by victims of domestic violence.

Many African Americans observed these snapshots and *more*. First and foremost they saw an adored and celebrated Black man forced to defend himself in a biased and broken criminal justice system. It is this image, with all of its historical weight, that resonated so deeply with African Americans—once again a Black man is accused of a crime by White folks—involving a White woman no less. For African Americans the issue of crime is intimately linked to the group's history and collective memory.

Simpson's case came to symbolize more than the plight of a fallen Black sports legend. Its impact was much bigger than that. In effect, O.J. became Nat Turner, Kunta Kinte, and Emmett Till, all rolled up into one person. What the community "saw" was a shackled O.J. At once, Simpson represented Black freedom fighters and the many unknown Black victims of America's racially discriminatory court system. Viewed through this lens, he was the latest in a long line of Black men who had been falsely accused by Whites of crimes against Whites, and who had been brought before the White court system. For many African Americans, Simpson's case presented just cause to take up the protest mantle. It represented Blacks standing up for their rights and fighting unjust charges. In this incarnation, Simpson represented each and every Black person. He became the stand-in for anyone who had been or knew someone who had been injured and abused by what Richard Pryor called not the justice system but the "just us" system.[35]

It might be tempting to dismiss the Simpson case as a product of its time, a case with little relevance today. The case, however, is timeless. In 2006, more than ten years following the not-guilty verdict, the Simpson case *still* pushes buttons. It still stands as the criminal trial that demonstrated, in a big way, that race still matters and that there is a huge racial divide in perceptions of justice. Today, though, it appears that fewer Blacks defend and support Simpson. However, many still believe the prosecution's case was weak and, therefore, they agree with the acquittal. A MSNBC 2004 poll found that 70 percent of African Americans believe Simpson was not guilty of the crimes. This is the same percentage of Blacks who supported Simpson in 1995. Pundits and comedians still comment on O.J. "getting away with murder." Simpson is still a tabloid staple, featured frequently on the front pages of the *National Enquirer*, *Star*, and *Globe*. His television interviews still attract large audiences.

In 2004, Katie Couric interviewed Simpson. In a wide-ranging conversation, Simpson maintained his innocence and expressed his opinion that Blacks and Whites have different perceptions of and experiences with the police. He said that Blacks are "more realistic" than Whites about the legal system because "Whites don't see the things that we (Blacks) see happen . . . cops will do things."[36] As a consequence, Blacks and Whites had vastly different responses to the not-guilty verdict.

The O.J. Simpson case attracted national and international attention and interest. However, in terms of what it represents to many African Americans, the case is just one in a large pool of lesser-known cases. The Black community's support for accused celebrities did not begin or end with O.J. As the discussion in the next section illustrates, O.J. is not alone. Simpson and his kin—other well-known Black men accused of crime—continue to evoke an ethos of Black protectionism.

O.J.'s Brothers

Although the Simpson case is unique in terms of interest, media focus, length of the trial, and outcome, it is not the first case to raise issues of Black protectionism. Among others, O.J. stands with Clarence Thomas, Marion Barry, Mike Tyson, Jesse Jackson, Michael Jackson, and Kobe Bryant. The details of these cases are thoroughly discussed later (see chapter 3). The Thomas confirmation hearings, which, like the Simpson case, you had to see to believe, merit early comment.

In 1991, following the retirement of Justice Thurgood Marshall, Clarence Thomas was nominated to the U.S. Supreme Court. Marshall was the first Black appointed to the Supreme Court. Questions were raised within the Black community and civil rights community about whether Thomas was a worthy successor to Marshall. African Americans appeared to be split. At the grassroots, many seemed to think Thomas was an acceptable choice. Many, however, while avoiding a close look at his record, concluded that if confirmed, he would "remember where he came from"—that he would act in the best interests of the common Black person.

Public support for Thomas solidified and increased once allegations of sexual harassment surfaced and after it became clear that the members of the Senate committee who would decide his fate were old, establishment White men. The hearing struck many as an eerily familiar attempt to bring down another Black man.

As was true for Simpson, Thomas received clear and solid support from African Americans. As was true for the Simpson case, it was unclear what benefit the African American community received for "loving Clarence." Together these cases raise similar issues and serve as a contemporary backdrop for the many issues raised by the application of Black protectionism. As established by the discussion in this chapter, the treatment of prominent African Americans is oft-times used as a watermark for assessing the overall progress of the race—a measure of how race relations have advanced over time.

Conclusion: Why Black Protectionism Matters

The above discussion lays the groundwork for this book's focus on Black protectionism. Protectionism answers "no" to the question of whether racial justice has been achieved, particularly in the criminal justice arena. The realities of Black life in America support the skepticism about racial progress that Black protectionism reflects.

Black athletes appear to have a unique role in the development and formation of contemporary uses of Black protectionism. Historically, Black sports figures, with their quest to compete on a level playing field with Whites, have represented the overall goal of Blacks to receive fair and just treatment in society. In this way, Black athletes and celebrities have been treated as representatives of the average Black person. Notably, the most popular cases involving Black protectionism have centered on Black men. In later chapters, I address how Black protectionism might be expanded to include African American woman and whether it should be extended to nonfamous Blacks as well.

Black protectionism is a practice that highlights racial injustices within the criminal justice system. Some strategies that are designed to promote racial justice are only available to select members of the African American community (e.g., lawyers who file civil rights law suits). All African Americans, however, can practice Black protectionism.

The shared perspectives and history of African Americans are at the core of Black protectionism. These common experiences have created a set of beliefs about how the justice system works. In turn, these belief systems have led to a cloak of armor—available to famous Blacks in trouble with the law. This racial shield appears to be widely available to famous Blacks, regardless of whether they identify themselves as Black, part-Black, or colorless.

Black protectionism expresses a basic sentiment. At the core it says Blacks should be treated fairly and equitably, particularly by the justice system. This includes the presumption of innocence, the right to a fair trial, and the right to procedural and substantive due process. In sum, it expresses that African Americans deserve the same protections as everyone else— equality before the law. The desire for basic human rights was concisely stated on sandwich-board signs worn by striking Black sanitation workers in 1968: "I am a man." This book offers an in-depth exploration of the who-what-when-why-and-how of Black protectionism. The bottom line is that Black protectionism matters because it points to the still-existing gap in life chances between African Americans and everyone else.

Library of Congress

CHAPTER TWO

DEEP ROOTS AND LONG BRANCHES

What's Wrong with This Picture?

Introduction

Where does Black protectionism come from? What keeps it going? This chapter explores the sources of Black support for fallen heroes. The discussion focuses on how it is that members of the Black community have come to hold some common perspectives and interpretations of how the world works regarding race relations. Many of the beliefs that Blacks share arise from their common background—historical and contemporary. This has led to the development of a collective consciousness based upon race-based experiences. It has shaped a Black cultural narrative—one based upon Blacks' shared history, shared space, and a shared sense of fairness. Each of these is further strengthened by the many anti-Black conspiracy theories that exist within the Black community.

The cultural narrative is the story Blacks tell about themselves—who they are and how they arrived where they are today. It presents a picture of a historically oppressed group, one that remains under racial siege, and one looking for answers to the question, *What's wrong with this picture?* The Black community's self-portrait forms a solid foundation for the development and promotion of Black protectionism—it practically demands a standard response to criminal allegations against members of the group, particularly those Blacks who have been successful. This chapter examines how the history of Blacks in the United States, their geographical proximity to one another, their use of conspiracies, their common perceptions of justice, and shared perceptions about how racial oppression works—separately and together—make the development of Black protectionism inevitable. The analysis supports the idea that many Blacks see their life opportunities as linked directly with the fate of the life opportunities for Blacks as a group. The concept of linked fate springs from the shared historical circumstances of African Americans and how these circumstances affect them—socially, economically, and politically.[1]

Shared History

Most Blacks living in the United States have ancestors who were held in chattel slavery on U.S. soil. This history includes enslavement, lynching, and legally sanctioned segregation in public places.[2] The oppression of Blacks did not occur in isolation—it was not limited to plantations and southern back roads. Each form of oppression was part of a much larger institutional and theoretical approach to Blacks, Blackness, and darker-skinned peoples in general.

The ravages of slavery cannot be overstated. Between ten and twenty million Black Africans were forcibly removed from their homeland and taken on a two-month journey across the Atlantic Ocean. In the first passage, European slave traders, or "slavers," traveled to Africa with iron, gunpowder, cloth, arms, and brandy, as trade goods to buy African men, women, and children. Once captured, Africans were chained, branded, and placed in ship holds. The future slaves were chained together in twos, by their feet and hands. During this Middle Passage, the slave cargo was bound and set like pieces on an immovable chessboard. In the final passage, slavers returned from the Americas back to England. There are wide-ranging estimates that between 10 and 70 percent of the captives did not survive the trip. By any calculation, however, millions of Africans did not complete the Middle Passage. Many died as a result of rampant diseases—including small pox, flu, and dysentery—resulting from grossly unsanitary conditions on the ships. Other Africans simply went mad. Some resisted capture and were killed. And, not surprisingly, some chose to jump overboard rather than continue on a brutal, destination-unknown, cross-Atlantic trek.[3] Those Africans who were still alive when they reached the New World's shores were subjected to punitive, inhumane, and alien living conditions. As vividly depicted in the independent film *Sankofa*, slaves were forced to perform back-breaking labor. They worked in the field, the kitchen, the bedroom, and on the road—in the sweltering sun, in the unrelenting rain, from daybreak to sundown.

What follows is a discussion of some of the social and cultural forms of racism—those that worked to maintain and reinforce White domination over enslaved Blacks. These social forces include theories of racial ranking, slave codes, lynching, the convict-lease and sharecropping systems, and Jim Crow.

Racial Ranking

During each historical stage of oppression—pre-slavery (prior to 1619), during slavery (1619–1865), and post-slavery (after 1865)—a key feature was the widespread belief that Blacks were intellectually inferior to Whites. In fact, some scientists argued that Blacks constituted a separate species from Whites. This thinking, known as polygenism, argued that each of the human races constitutes a separate biological species—each originating from a different Adam. Another school of thought was monogenism, which argued that all humans were members of the same biological species. By either theory, Blacks were considered inferior and justifiably enslaved.

In his book, *The Mismeasure of Man*, Stephen Jay Gould documents the vast research done by scientists who sought to "prove" Black inferiority. One of the premier nineteenth-century polygenists was Louis Agassiz, a Swiss naturalist who became a Harvard professor. His work advocated racial ranking, which placed Blacks at the bottom rung of the intelligence ladder. Agassiz argued that one's innate ability should determine his level of education. According to Agassiz, Blacks were mentally deficient and were properly relegated to manual labor and should be separated from Whites. His theorizing was not based on hard data culled from rigorous and replicated scientific trials. Instead, it was based upon his uncomfortable first encounters with Blacks in America. He was appalled by the physical distinctions between Blacks and Whites. He was convinced that differences in skin color, hair texture, and body structure were proof of the different biological origins of Blacks and Whites. Agassiz was one of many White scientists who attempted to mask his racist preconceptions with a scientific gloss.[4]

Samuel Morton was another nineteenth-century scientist who sought to examine racial difference. He chose to study the link between brain size and intelligence. To test his hypothesis that Blacks had smaller brains, and thus were less intelligent than Whites, Morton collected more than eight hundred skulls and measured their cranial capacity. His study included the skulls of Caucasians, American Indians, and Blacks. Morton concluded that Blacks had smaller brains than Whites. A review of his findings, however, revealed numerous research flaws. Scientists who later reviewed his work discovered that he had fudged some of his results. Further, Morton failed to consider other possible explanations for his findings, including the possibility that brain size is correlated with body size, not intelligence. He was so intent on establishing that Blacks were intellectually inferior to Whites that he did not see the fallacy of his own reasoning. According to Morton's own hypothesis, elephants would have to be considered more intelligent than human beings.[5]

From either perspective—polygenism or monogenism—Blacks were not and could not be on par with Whites. These theories represented the prevailing ideology and were used to justify the enslavement and maltreatment of Africans brought to America. These racist ideologies were also aided by and interlinked with the existing laws and religious doctrines.

Slave Codes, Black Laws, and the Courts

Given the mainstream antebellum view of Black inferiority combined with the "peculiar institution"[6] of slavery, it is no surprise that the written law offered neither solace nor relief to Blacks. In meticulous detail, the slave codes spelled out the law on Black movement in the slave territories. These harsh codes, first adopted in Virginia, regulated slaved life from sun up to sun down. Here are some representative examples:

- Because slaves were real estate, they could not inherit or own property, including pets.

- Slaves could not be parties in a civil case, nor could they testify in a civil or criminal case against someone White.

- Male slaves were prohibited from gathering in groups of eight or more.

- Slaves could not use "abusive" language toward Whites.

- Slaves were not permitted to preach.

Whites who sought to undermine the institution of slavery were also subject to code violations. For instance, those who taught Blacks to read or tried to help them escape faced harsh penalties under the law.

Black laws operated in the free states and were in effect at the same time as the slave codes. They were designed to regulate and restrict the comings, goings, and doings of Blacks in the North. Ohio took the lead in passing Black laws. The legislation designated, among other things, where Blacks could live; the bond amount they had to post to begin a trade; the taxes they had to pay for education (although they were not permitted to attend school); the fee charged for entering the state; when Blacks could testify in court (they were prohibited from testifying in court against someone White); and their ineligibility for office (civil or military).

Antebellum-era cases, such as *Dred Scott v. Sandford*,[7] upheld the mainstream White view that Blacks were inferior—a view that offered no relief for the enslaved.[8] Those Blacks who managed to step onto free soil were still not free. In the 1857 *Dred Scott* decision, the Supreme Court held that Scott, a slave, who was moved from Missouri, a slave state, to Illinois, a free state, was not entitled to the protections granted by either the Constitution or the Declaration of Independence. In fact, the Court stated, Blacks are of such an "inferior order" that they have "no rights which the white man was bound to respect."[9]

Both the Emancipation Proclamation, signed in 1863, and the end of the Civil War, in 1865, are widely cited as officially ending slavery. However, they did little to actually free the masses of enslaved Blacks. In a compromise with the Confederacy, the Proclamation was riddled with territorial exceptions. Further, notice of "freedom" was so sketchy that many slaves did not initially learn of its existence. Juneteenth is a holiday that celebrates the actual end of slavery. On June 19, 1865, *two and one-half years after* Lincoln signed the Emancipation Proclamation, slaves in Galveston, Texas, learned from Union soldiers that the war had ended. They were the last slaves who were set free.

Lynching

With the horrors of slavery still fresh in their minds, newly emancipated slaves were subjected to mob murders by Whites. Lynchings took many forms, including shooting, drawing and quartering, stabbing, burning, and hanging. Lynchings were not simple killings. They involved a ritualized set of activities. The lynch victim was kidnapped (sometimes from a jail cell). The mob—which often included local lawmen—had to select the location. A method of killing had to be chosen and a time of death had to be set. These vigilante public executions were often celebrated as community events. It was not unusual for newspapers to run notices of upcoming lynchings. Depending on the notoriety of the alleged crime, a lynching might attract a few or a few thousand spectators. In many instances the victim's feet and hands were bound and their faces were covered. The lynch victim was then subject to multiple whippings and mutilation—often skinned before being killed.

Although official estimates place the number of lynchings between the end of the Civil War and through the Civil Rights era at approximately four thousand, historians, including antilynching crusader Ida B. Wells, estimate the number to be much higher, closer to ten thousand.[10] Between 1882 and 1899 alone, the *Chicago Tribune* reported that 2,533 Blacks were lynched by White mobs.[11]

Lynching has been primarily an interracial crime—one involving vigilante Whites who hunt down and kill Blacks. The primary victims of lynching have been Black men. Designed as a tool to keep Blacks in line, lynch mobs took action to prevent Blacks from achieving equal status with Whites. The common trigger for a lynch mob was Black activity that was considered to threaten the White hierarchy. Unproven allegations were sufficient to instigate a lynching. Beyond rumors that a Black person had committed a serious crime (e.g., rape, robbery, barn burning, or murder), many other circumstances could set a lynch mob in motion:

- The acquittal of a Black man accused of committing a crime against someone White;

- "Incendiarism";[12]

- Allegations that a Black person had been "saucy" (disrespectful) to someone White;

- Rumors that a Black man had made lewd overtures to a White woman;

- Being related to a Black person suspected of committing a crime.

Although ostensibly designed as a practice to protect the virtue of White womanhood, lynching was widely used to enforce and reinforce White domination. Assault, not rape, was the most common rationale Whites gave for lynching Blacks.

The prevalence and brutality of lynchings sent a clear message to Blacks—step out of place and you will experience a cruel fate. The frequency of lynchings in the South prompted many Black families to move North and West. Lynchings, however, were not limited to the South—they took place in every region of the country. The book, *Without Sanctuary: Lynching Photography in America*, vividly illustrates the lynching ceremony.[13] More than eighty photographs document that lynching was both a ritual and a sport—one that was well planned and well attended by White community members—a public act of community vengeance. Further, while many lynchings were of individuals, many involved groups—groups of men or families. Sometimes lynch victims were old Black men.

Orlando Patterson's work details the lynching ceremony. He describes the rush to collect the victim's body parts after the lynching was complete. Onlookers fought over fingers, toes, teeth, and pieces of flesh. Some caught pieces of the lynch victim's clothing—torn off and thrown to the crowd before the killing. Others settled for purchasing photos of the lynching, often sold and used as postcards. Describing lynching as "ritual cannibalism," Patterson discusses cases in which the victim was forced to eat some of his own body parts before being hanged, knifed, or burned. Another prominent feature of the practice was the smell of burning flesh. Patterson highlights the "profound religious significance" of lynching—particularly for Southerners.[14]

Convict-Lease, Sharecropping, and Vagrancy Laws

The end of slavery was met with new forms of Black oppression. The convict-lease and sharecropper systems led to the reenslavement of many Blacks. Under the convict-lease system, Blacks who had been imprisoned were leased out for hard labor. This built up state coffers and created a financial interest for states—encouraging them to maintain a sizeable prison population.

The sharecropping regime resembled slavery in that Blacks worked for Whites on their farms. Newly freed but without the promised forty acres, Blacks were forced into a new form of servitude under Whites. Blacks tilled White farm lands and at year's end were required to pay off their debts to the landowner (e.g., for equipment, fertilizer, seed, food, and shelter). This system was set up in such a way that it was virtually impossible for Blacks to escape the cycle of debt. Rather than operating as a method for Blacks to save money and buy their own property, many Southern Blacks were forced to sharecrop for decades with no other way to pay off existing debts. In fact, there are written accounts stating that there were still Black sharecroppers working on White southern lands through the late twentieth century.[15]

Vagrancy laws enhanced the convict-lease system. In essence these laws allowed Blacks to be placed in jail for being Black and unemployed. For instance, Mississippi's statute, passed immediately following on the heels of the Civil War, made it illegal for "freedmen, free negroes and mulattoes . . . with no lawful employment or business" to gather.[16] Violators were subject to a fine and imprisonment. Thus, an increase in arrests for vagrancy meant an increase in the pool of eligible convict-lease workers. Some states took full advantage of this by boosting their Black prison population. In Texas, for instance, Blacks, who made up 25 percent of the state's population, comprised 50 percent of those in prison. The convict-lease system was adopted in states across the South. It provided cash-poor states with an economic incentive to incarcerate—through the system, inmates were forced to pay for the cost of their incarceration.

Jim Crow

The segregation statutes of the twentieth century were an updated version of the Black codes. These laws operated to control the life circumstances and living conditions of the daughters and sons of former slaves. Jim Crow enforced the concept of racialized spaces—some places were reserved for Whites only, others were relegated to Blacks. A short list of spaces that were segregated throughout the South includes: buses, trains, public restrooms, courthouses, movie theaters, prisons, parks, swimming pools, cemeteries, water fountains, doctors' waiting rooms, and hospital wards. Jim Crow not only determined who could go where, but who could interact with whom. Segregation statutes made marriage and cohabitation between Blacks and Whites illegal; required separate schools for Blacks and Whites; established separate facilities for Black prisoners and White prisoners (including juveniles); prescribed Black ministers to officiating at ceremonies for Blacks only; and required separate military battalions for Blacks and Whites.[17] The social, political, economic, and legal systems were aligned to deny Blacks basic human rights. It is no surprise that this common history has generated a unique, race-based collective consciousness for Blacks.

Shared Space

Although racist laws mandating racial segregation in public places have been officially outlawed, vestiges remain. In urban areas, where more than 90 percent of Blacks live, there are still Black sections of town—think of Washington, D.C., Detroit, Chicago, New York, and Los Angeles. Consider who lives in the sections of cities with schools and streets named for Martin Luther King Jr., Rosa Parks, Benjamin Banneker, George Washington Carver, and other Black leaders.

In many places, Blacks and Whites are still divided by train tracks, rivers, and industrial plants. A contemporary look at residential housing patterns dramatically illustrates the impact of these race-based policies and practices. In *American Apartheid*,[18] Douglas Massey and Nancy Denton use 1990 Census tract statistics to explore residential patterns by race.[19] Their research indicates that African Americans are not only segregated, they are hypersegregated: Most Blacks live in racially isolated clusters, away from other racial groups.[20] These stark housing patterns were found in most major metropolitan centers, where more than 80 percent of Blacks live, including Atlanta, Baltimore, Chicago, Detroit, Los Angeles, New York, and Philadelphia.[21] A study based on the 2000 Census, conducted almost ten years later, reported similar findings.[22] Whites live in neighborhoods that are 80 percent White and Blacks live in neighborhoods that are 75 percent Black.[23] Cincinnati, Cleveland, Detroit, Miami, Newark, and New York are among the cities with the largest number of segregated neighborhoods.

Residential segregation did not just happen. Twentieth-century policies and practices, by the government, private businesses, and individuals, included housing restrictions in the form of restrictive covenants, redlining, and racial steering.[24] Racially restrictive covenants prohibited the sale of property to Blacks (and other groups of color). Although today it is unconstitutional, racially restrictive language still exists in some property transactions. Blacks were also denied access to programs including the Home Owners' Loan Corporation, making it harder to secure home mortgage loans. Between 1930 and 1960 Blacks held less than 1 percent of all U.S. mortgages. Until the 1960s, the Federal Housing Authority (FHA) financed homes in White suburban areas. At the same time the FHA routinely denied loans in urban markets, where most Blacks resided.[25]

The density and shape of a racial group's residential community has implications for its social community. It determines whether the social community will be a tightly knit one. People who live closer to one another are more likely to remain in closer contact, particularly when they are concentrated in certain cities and certain communities. The relatively small size of the Black community—13 percent of the U.S. population—enhances its ability to remain close. Its shared history and space have helped to create a race-based community—one with its own identity. To some degree, individual identities are muted and the group may be seen and increasingly view itself as part of a collective. Thus, an attack on one member of the group, especially a successful, high-profile member, may be thought of as an attack upon the entire group. When one member of the group is under the public microscope, such as O.J. Simpson, that person becomes a stand-in for the entire community of Black people.

It is worth noting that most of the famous Blacks who have received Black protectionism, such as Simpson and Clarence Thomas (see chapter 3) do not reside in the typical, segregated Black community. Interestingly, however, many famous Blacks were raised in predominantly Black areas. This dynamic raises a number of issues. First, who is "in" the Black community?—does it require physical presence, or is being Black, regardless of where you live, enough? Second, even if a famous Black person lives within the Black community, are they *entitled* to Black protectionism—regardless of their community service or politics? (See chapters 5 and 6.)

One contemporary manifestation of African American cultural memory—symbolized by a common history and close living quarters—is a deep distrust of the criminal justice system.[26] There is widespread knowledge that the legal system has been and continues to disproportionately punish African Americans.

The history and space shared by African Americans shapes the community's view of its lawbreakers. Regina Austin observes that whether the

Black community defends those who break the law depends upon considerations that others, outside the community, may not take into account.[27] The "Black community evaluates behavior in terms of its impact on the overall progress of the race. Black criminals are pitied, praised, protected, emulated, or embraced if their behavior has a positive impact on the social, political and economic well-being of Black communal life."[28]

One outcome of the historically racist treatment that African Americans have faced in the United States is that they have been subjected to more than a century of residential segregation. As the next section details, this forced isolation and discrimination has fostered the group's development of various underground theories and explanations of White racism.

Conspiracies

Conspiracy theories are a fact of life within the African American community. They are communicated and discussed at the barbershop, at the beauty parlor, on the radio, at parties, at the day spa, on the phone, at church, over the Internet, and on the street—wherever Black people congregate. Conspiracies deal with issues both large and small. They may arise to explain the dearth of Black academy award winners. Or, they may focus on more serious questions, such as why Blacks are still at the "bottom of the well"[29]—e.g., double-digit rates of unemployment, low rates of high school graduation, poor health, high rates of imprisonment, and low income and assets (see chapter 1). At the core, many of the conspiracies seek to address why Blacks, 140 years after the end of the Civil War and 50 years after the Supreme Court's decision in *Brown v. Board of Education*, are still caught holding the proverbial bag. These anti-Black conspiracies—ones that suggest that there are social forces aligned to keep Blacks down—challenge the idea that Blacks are primarily at fault for their marginal status. In a nutshell, these conspiracies blame White oppression *today*, for the continued marginality of Blacks.

Studies that look at how conspiracies work within the Black community show that they serve as tracking devices to locate and label White oppression. In her book, *I Heard It through the Grapevine*, Patricia Turner discusses the various conspiracy theories operating within the Black community.[30] Turner observes that Blacks are not the only racial group that utilizes conspiracies. Whites, too, have race-based conspiracies. She notes, however, that discussions of conspiracies in the African American community are more likely to be private. Turner's research also shows that conspiracies are not new—they date back more than four hundred years. The book traces the chronology of conspiracies that have circulated within the African American community. As the author observes, rumors address issues large and small, including topics that explain relations among Blacks and between Blacks and Whites. Many of the more popular ones fall under the category of plots by the U.S. government to destroy the Black man or the Black race.[31] The widespread belief in conspiracies is not surprising when we consider some historical realities, such as the Tuskegee syphilis experiment—a study in which dozens of unwitting Blacks were used as guinea pigs, to examine the effects of syphilis on the human body.

One of the more widespread contemporary rumors circulating within the Black community came in the aftermath of hurricane Katrina. Many believed that the slow response to the hurricane ravaged Louisiana victims was due to the fact that most survivors were Black and poor. Some suggested that the federal government's malign neglect was designed to ensure that thousands of Blacks died, killed one another, or were killed by national guardsmen.[32] The belief that crack cocaine was intentionally spread in Black communities and that the HIV/AIDS virus was invented as a form of genocide against African Americans are also contemporary community rumors.

Turner identifies two kinds of drug-related conspiracies: malicious intent and benign neglect.[33] Malicious intent conspiracies are based on the belief that there is a specific plan in operation. An example of a malicious intent conspiracy is the belief that crack cocaine was intentionally planted in urban areas to kill off the Black community.[34] Benign neglect conspiracies are those that do not require intent to harm; rather, the harm is caused by the government's failure to protect members of the African American community.[35] Slow response times by the police in answering calls for service in Black neighborhoods, and the failure of the government to prevent the influx of drugs into urban areas, are examples of benign neglect conspiracies. Turner argues that conspiracy theories within the Black community "function as tools of resistance." This view links to an argument raised by Regina Austin. She suggests that anti-Black conspiracy theories serve a functional purpose.[36] They act as a critical response to the social and political marginalization of Blacks by mainstream institutions. Austin states:

> [Anti-black conspiracies] circulat[e] through available channels not controlled by the dominant white society. . . . Through theorizing, blacks express what they are concerned about in a way that is unmediated by the strictures of conventional reporting. . . . [T]he theories come close to being free, uncensored speech. There is a logic and a rationality to many anti-black conspiracy theories. Although they sometimes have a fantastic quality, the theories offer explanations at a time when bad things are happening to blacks and no one is adequately explaining why.[37]

Austin's examination reveals why conspiracy theories are so popular. Viewed as a kind of "deviant discourse,"[38] conspiracies refute the mainstream picture of idealized race relations. They provide an opposing narrative for Blacks—one that reaffirms the lived experiences of African Americans. In this way they "create solidarity and facilitate mass mobilization."[39] Conspiracies support actions by Blacks that protect them against the onslaught of White racism. This includes Black protectionism. Overall, the creation of conspiracy theories is a predictable response and a useful instrument for historically oppressed racial groups.[40]

In a study that raises issues related to Austin's research, Theodore Sasson conducted peer group interviews to test the prevalence of Black conspiracy theories.[41] In his 1995 research, based on small-group meetings with fifty-one adults, Sasson found that conspiracies serve two functions. First, they are used to make sense of disproportionately high rates of social dysfunction (e.g., arrest and conviction rates). Second, they promote in-group solidarity by reinforcing a shared historical narrative. As well, Sasson found that conspiracies are usually discussed in vague terms. The perceived conspirators are an interchangeable group of villains—including the police, the media, and White society in general. Sasson concludes that because there is little room in the public discourse for acknowledging the impact of White racism on Black life, many Blacks perceive that there is a wide and vast array of potential conspirators.[42]

Overall, conspiracies have wide appeal within the Black community. They act as frequent reminders of both past and current racial injustices. They also act to highlight White racism as the primary cause of what has been labeled dysfunction in the Black community.

Being Labeled a Social Problem

The research on social problems helps to explain the popularity of conspiracies and more generally the popularity of Black protectionism. Studies of social problems explore how groups define a situation as a problem and how they then take steps to solve the problem.[43] Disproportionately high rates of Black arrests, large numbers of convictions for crack cocaine, and exceptionally high incarceration rates for Black men are social problems that affect the African American community. Within society, these are used as examples of why Blacks are a group with marginal status.

One way of thinking about Black protectionism is to see it as the Black community's response to being labeled deviant. In other words, the Black community's reaction to being labeled a social problem has been to dismiss that very labeling as a social problem. The belief held by many African Americans, that they are viewed as a problem group, is based upon many factors, including their direct and indirect experiences with the justice system.[44] This perception is enhanced by the standard media portrayal of African Americans as outsiders, as troublemakers—images that emphasize overinvolvement in the criminal justice system—and a laundry list of other negative social facts, such as high rates of out-of-wedlock births, high-school dropouts, single-parent households, infant mortality, and unemployment.

Closely tied to the response to being a social problem is the problem of racial stigma—specifically the negative social stigma that attaches to Blackness. Stigma refers to more than being stereotyped or subjected to racial slurs—it refers to being a member of a group that has not achieved full acceptance within society, a group that is disfavored and dishonored.[45] Being part of a group with a racial stigma means having two identities, a virtual one (the one that society and the media says you have) and an actual one. The problem with the virtual label is that it is based on assumptions, not facts, and as a consequence it usually varies greatly from one's actual social identity. Given that the racial stigma applies to Blacks as a group, it is not surprising that it would provoke a group response—such as Black protectionism.

Blacks as a group are burdened with a negative race stigma and have been labeled a social problem. This, in addition to the community's disproportionately high rate of social marginality, is directly tied to America's history of racism. Black protectionism operates as a buffer to America's racist history. It arises as a natural and arguably rational response to being negatively labeled.

Cultural resistance may help explain Blacks' rejection of negative social labels. African Americans refuse to be labeled as a social problem and to be treated as having a negative racial stigma. Theories of cultural resistance argue that groups adopt oppositional cultures and practices in response to mainstream values that perpetuate social injustice and power inequities. Acts of cultural resistance are evident in how a community responds to crime and its lawbreakers. Rejection of society's norms of justice may be blatant or subtle. For oppressed groups, the resistance tends to be underground—because more open forms of protest are likely to be met with large-scale resistance by the government.[46] If viewed as a form of cultural resistance, Black protectionism reflects a decision by Blacks to refuse the criminal label placed on numerous Black celebrities. It is a way in which Blacks can register their protest against long-standing racial injustices. Like conspiracies, this below-the-radar strategy may be a "weapon of the weak,"[47] but it represents a powerful community statement about the connection between America's history of racism and the contemporary conditions of African Americans.

A Shared Sense of Fairness

For African Americans, a communal sense of fairness flows directly from the groups' common history and shared space. The belief in fairness is not only a statement that Blacks have rights, too; it acknowledges that Blacks have and continue to experience a double standard of justice. African Americans take note of their personal experiences within the justice system and the experiences of other African Americans—friends, family members, acquaintances, colleagues, strangers, and Blacks in the news. Black sensitivity to racial injustices within the justice system is heightened by the fact that many Blacks stand within one or two degrees of someone—sibling, parent, child, cousin, or friend—who is in prison or in some other way caught in the justice system (e.g., parole or probation).[48] Further, Blacks also consider what role racial bias plays in criminal and noncriminal cases involving Blacks, compared with Whites.

Conclusion

The history of Blacks in this country is closely linked with the Black community's sense of mistreatment and isolation. This history includes racist theories of Black inferiority, cases and legislation that enforce these views, vigilante lynching rituals, and constantly evolving forms of reenslavement. Together, these are strong building blocks in creating a Black perspective on Whites and racism. These entrenched views have become further cemented because most Blacks live in predominantly Black communities. Most Blacks live, work, and socialize around other Blacks and share a common story and a common set of experiences. Not surprisingly in a climate of shared experience and shared space, conspiracy theories flourish. Rumors of racist attacks on Blacks allow the community to create its own explanation of race relations and not simply blame itself for all of its problems. Finally, all these factors have created a community that has a common view of what fairness and justice are and whether they exist.

Together these shared realities—history, space, and perceptions of justice—support and in fact predict the development of Black protectionism. Black protectionism appears to operate as a form of racial resistance. It shows the Black community—through communal will and communal interest—as rejecting mainstream attempts to decide what constitutes African American deviance. It is a form of Black self-determination.[49] So, in answer to the question, *What's wrong with this picture?* the Black community's loud response is *Racism*. Now that the historical backdrop and sources of Black protectionism have been identified, we can look at how Black protectionism works by examining contemporary cases of its application.

CLARENCE THOMAS, O.J. SIMPSON, JESSE JACKSON, AND R. KELLY: STRANGE BEDFELLOWS

Introduction

Black protectionism is everywhere. Hardly a season passes without a prominent Black person being accused of a crime. Allegations run the gamut. They include felonies, low-level misdemeanors, and charges of inappropriate remarks. The potential for Black protectionism exists every time there is a serious charge leveled against a high-profile African American.

Table 3.1 lists cases involving some of the potential recipients of Black protectionism. It includes the alleged criminal or unethical conduct, year of the charge, the person's title, and the outcome of their case (where available). Each of the thirty-four cases, most occurring during the period from 1994 through 2004, received national attention (for more detail see the appendix). Five cases occurred prior to 1994 (O.J. Simpson, Clarence Thomas, Mike Tyson, Lani Guinier, and Carol Moseley-Braun). These cases are included on the list because of their significance in framing and analyzing Black protectionism. The list includes athletes, religious leaders, elected officials, entertainers, politicians, cabinet members, businessmen, and civil rights leaders. In most instances, the alleged criminal conduct involves white-collar crime, such as fraud, embezzlement, or bribery. Some cases, however, involve violent crime, such as rape or homicide. A small number involve what some might label "victimless" crime, such as drug use.

The cases are divided into four categories for discussion; those involving political officials; Black women; sexual assault; and athletes and rappers.[1] After reviewing the cases, it was determined that these categories provided a useful framework for examining how Black protectionism works. In some instances, a case may fit into a single category. For those cases included within the discussion, there is a detailed overview of facts, the reaction by the Black community (where available) how the case compares with others in the category, and the outcome of the case.[2] The discussion of Black protectionism is limited to incidents involving well-known Blacks, so that the perspectives of the Black community as a group can be considered. Case information was gathered from various sources, including national newspapers, the Internet, books, magazines, journal articles, national polls, and Black media outlets.

At the outset, there are two additional categories of cases that deserve note. First, there are some cases that are technically eligible for Black protectionism but unlikely to trigger it. First, there are cases involving prominent African Americans who are known to have repeated run-ins with the law, such as Bobby Brown and James Brown. They are included in table 3.1. Second, there are low-level crimes that carry minimal social stigma and little possibility of jail time. Incidents falling into the second category are not included in the table or in the following discussion. For instance, well-known Blacks who have been arrested for possession of marijuana—e.g., Dionne Warwick, Whitney Houston, and NBA players Chris Webber and Damon Stoudamire—are not listed in table 3.1. Notably, in both types of cases, the charges do not appear to be taken very seriously and are more likely to be the butt of jokes on morning drive radio shows and late night television.

Table 3.2 lists the operating mechanisms for Black protectionism. The first is that an allegation of wrongdoing can be established by either an accusation of criminal or unethical conduct. The second requirement is that the allegation must be made against someone Black. Third, the charge must come from outside the Black community, from a mainstream agent (e.g., district attorney, congressional committee, or law enforcement). Finally, the allegation must be made against someone with a national reputation or credibility as a racial spokesperson (someone who is recognized as a voice on issues important to the Black community).

Table 3.3 lists the "trigger questions" for Black protectionism. These questions show the contrasting reactions between Whites and Blacks in their responses to allegations of criminal behavior against well-known African Americans. As suggested by the queries, Whites appear to respond

Table 3.1. Potential Recipients of Black Protectionism, 1994–2004 (34 cases)

Name	Year	Allegation	Position	Outcome
Anthony Anderson	2004	Rape	Actor	Case dismissed
Ron Artest	2004	Assault & Battery	NBA	Criminal case pending; Suspension from NBA
Marion Barry*	1990	Drug Use	Mayor, Washington, D.C.	Convicted: Misdemeanor (6 mos. prison)
Bobby Brown	2003	Assault	Entertainer	Pending
James Brown	2004	Assault	Entertainer	Pending
Kobe Bryant	2003	Rape	NBA	Case dismissed
Bill Campbell	2004	Corruption; Tax Evasion	Mayor, Atlanta	Pending
Rae Carruth	1999	Murder	NFL	Convicted; 19–24 yrs. in prison
Ben Chavis	1994	Sexual Harassment	NAACP Executive	Settled out of court, removed from post
Bill Clinton	1998	Adultery; Perjury; Obstruction of Justice	President	Impeached & Acquitted
Sean "Diddy" Combs	1999	Weapons Charges; Bribery	Music Entrepreneur	Acquitted
Bill Cosby	1997	Adultery	Entertainer	Admission
Joycelyn Elders	1994	Inappropriate Remarks	U.S. Surgeon General	Resigned from post
Michael Espy	1994	Corruption	Secretary of Agriculture	Acquitted

(continued)

Table 3.1. *(Continued)*

Name	Year	Allegation	Position	Outcome
Lani Guinier*	1993	Inappropriate Writings	Law Professor	Nomination withdrawn
Alexis Herman	1998	Corruption	Secretary of Labor	No charges filed
Allen Iverson	2002	Assault	NBA	Charges dropped
Janet Jackson	2004	Indecency	Music Entrepreneur	No charges filed
Jesse Jackson	2001	Adultery; Fathering Child Outside Marriage	Director, Rainbow/PUSH	Apologized
Michael Jackson	2003	Sexual Assault	Entertainer	Acquitted
R. Kelly	2002	Rape	Entertainer	Pending
Ray Lewis	2000	Murder	NFL	Pled guilty to obstruction of justice; 1 yr. probation
Lisa "Left Eye" Lopes	1994	Arson	Entertainer	Pled guilty, fined and sentenced to 5 yrs. probation and alcohol rehabilitation
Henry Lyons	1997	Adultery; Corruption	Reverend, National Baptist Convention	Convicted: 5½-yr. sentence
Carol Moseley-Braun*	1992	Misappropriation of funds	U.S. Congress	No charges filed
Hazel O'Leary	1996	Corruption	Secretary of Energy	No charges filed

Melvin Reynolds	1995	Sexual assault	U.S. Congress	Convicted: 6½-yr. sentence (released after 3 yrs.)
Diana Ross	2002	DUI	Music Entrepreneur	48 hours in jail; 1-yr. unsupervised probation
O.J. Simpson*	1994	Murder	NFL	Acquitted
Latrell Sprewell	1997	Assault	NBA	Fined & Suspended
John Street	2003	Corruption	Mayor, Philadelphia	No charges filed
Clarence Thomas*	1991	Sexual Harassment	U.S. Supreme Court nominee	Nomination confirmed
Mike Tyson*	1992	Rape	Boxer	Convicted: 3 yrs. prison
Jayson Williams	2002	Aggravated Manslaughter	NBA	Acquitted, felony; convicted, misdemeanor

*Pre-1994 cases.

Table 3.2. Operating Mechanisms for Black Protectionism

1. An allegation of wrongdoing
2. Against someone Black
3. By a mainstream agent
4. Made against someone with a national reputation or credibility as racial spokesperson

Table 3.3. Trigger Questions for Black Protectionism

For Blacks	For Whites
1. Did he commit the offense?	1. Did he commit the offense?
2. Even if he did, was he set up?	
3. Would he risk everything he has (e.g., wealth, fame, material possessions) to commit an offense?	
4. Is he the only person who has committed the offense?	
5. Do Whites accused of committing the offense receive the same scrutiny and treatment?	
6. Is the accusation part of a plot to destroy the Black race?	

differently than Blacks upon learning that a high-profile African American has been accused of a crime.

The next section of this chapter details the range of cases involving Black protectionism—where it has been applied and where it might have been used to protect and defend a prominent African American charged with criminal or unethical activity.

Political Officials

Historically, the African American community has revered its political leadership, especially its elected representatives. This reverence is partly a testament to historical and contemporary roadblocks placed in the path of would-be Black politicians and voters. Today for example, national-level Black politicians face particular challenges.[3] Studies consistently indicate that Whites are less inclined to vote for Black politicians. Since 1965, when the Voting Rights Act was passed, Douglass Wilder has been the only African American elected governor, and Carol Moseley-Braun, Edward Brooke, and Barack Obama, the only elected Black senators. At the local level, however, there have been increases in the number of Black elected officials.[4]

The case of Adam Clayton Powell offers a history lesson and serves as a starting point for this discussion. His case sheds light on the reasons for the Black community's protective embrace of fallen political leaders.

With their entry into electoral politics, Black leaders faced heightened scrutiny and abuse.[5] In 1944, Powell was elected as the congressional representative for Harlem.[6] A few years into his term, he came under attack because he did not support Adlai Stevenson, who was heading the Democrat's presidential ticket.[7] Stevenson had minimized the importance of a civil rights amendment and refused to meet with Powell and other congressmen to discuss his position.[8] In 1953, following the election of Dwight Eisenhower as president, Powell was charged with tax evasion. The government's $3,000 tax evasion lawsuit against Powell was costly in both time and money.[9] Following his embrace of the Black power movement, Powell was removed from Congress in 1967, by a vote of 364 to 64.[10] His case went before the U.S. Supreme Court, which decided that he had been wrongly removed from office.[11] Powell ran again for Congress in 1970 and lost to another Black politician, Charles Rangel.[12]

The Powell case provides a dramatic illustration of the difficulties faced by some Black politicians. The government has engaged in an intense and prolonged surveillance and suppression of Black progressive, grassroots, and radical organizations, including the NAACP, Southern Christian Leadership Conference, the Student Nonviolent Coordinating Committee, and the Black Panther Party.[13] This harsh reality partly explains the strong support that Black politicians receive from the Black community. With this history in mind, it is not surprising that Black politicians are generally granted protectionism.[14]

Marion Barry

The case involving former Washington, D.C., mayor Marion Barry offers an interesting application of Black protectionism. In January 1990, Barry was captured on videotape in a D.C. hotel room, with a woman who was not his wife, smoking a crack pipe. The FBI used Barry's former girlfriend, Hazel Diane Moore, to lure him to the hotel suite.[15] Moore, who agreed to participate in the sting, was paid $1,700 a month by the FBI.[16] The eighty-three-minute videotape indicates that Barry was as interested in having sex with Moore as he was in using drugs.[17] The fact that Barry's criminal conduct was captured on videotape sets his case apart from others: It is beyond dispute that Barry actually engaged in criminal activity. Barry was convicted of misdemeanor drug possession and acquitted of one count of drug possession. There was a hung jury on twelve other counts, including perjury.[18]

As indicated by the trigger questions (table 3.3, question 2), the racial target's guilt or innocence is not decisive in determining whether Black protectionism applies. This is evident in the Black community's response to Barry's arrest and prosecution. Many Blacks believed that the mayor had gone to Moore's room for a sexual liaison, not to smoke crack cocaine. The central focus in Barry's case was not the first trigger question, but the second and sixth questions. The emphasis shifted from, "Did he commit the offense?" to "Even if he did, was he set up?" and "Is this accusation part of a government conspiracy to destroy the Black race?" The Barry case suggests that Black protectionism acts to minimize criminal charges that Blacks view as overreaching by the state or federal government.

In 1991, after serving a six-month term in federal prison, Barry returned to Washington, D.C. He moved to Anacostia, the predominantly Black and mostly poor southeast quadrant of Washington. The following year, Barry ran for city council and won by a landslide. In 1994 Barry ran for mayor for a fourth time and won. It was a stunning and unprecedented victory. Following this, Congress stripped the D.C. mayor's office of some of its powers. In 2004, Barry was reelected to the D.C. city council.

Melvin Reynolds

In 1995, Reynolds, an Illinois congressman and Rhodes Scholar, was charged with having sex with Beverly Heard, a minor.[19] The sixteen-year-old Heard was a campaign volunteer. At that time, Reynolds was already under investigation for election campaign violations.[20] Although Reynolds denied any physical contact with Heard, he admitted to engaging with her in "phone sex." A jury convicted the married congressman of criminal sexual assault, child pornography, obstruction of justice, and aggravated criminal sexual abuse.[21] In a separate case, Reynolds faced charges of corruption and fraud. In 1997, Reynolds was sentenced to six and a half years in federal prison.[22]

The reaction to this case mirrored, to a lesser degree, the reaction to the Barry incident. Very few sought to justify Reynolds's actions. The focus shifted away from his involvement (table 3.3, question 1) to both the *actions* of the federal prosecutor's office against him and the *inactions* of the federal prosecutor's office against other (non-Black) elected officials (fifth trigger question). For example, some described the prosecutors as over-zealous in Reynolds's case. Others referred to the case of former Oregon senator Bob Packwood as proof that Reynolds was being held to a different, more punitive standard. Packwood had been accused of sexually assaulting more than two dozen female staffers during his congressional tenure.[23] In 1995, Packwood resigned and faced no criminal charges.[24]

Bill Clinton: "The First Black President"

Arguably the most provocative and controversial recipient of Black protectionism has been former president Bill Clinton.[25] Within the Black community, Clinton has been, in many ways, referred to and treated as an African American. Social commentators, from Nobel laureate Toni Morrison to comedian Chris Rock,[26] have referenced Clinton's "Black" skin.[27] In a 1998 piece in *The New Yorker*, Morrison details the racialized treatment Clinton received from the mainstream press:

> White skin notwithstanding, this is our first Black president. Blacker than any actual person who could be elected in our children's lifetime . . . Clinton displays almost every trope of Blackness: single parent household, born poor, working-class, saxophone-playing, McDonald's and junk-food loving boy from Arkansas.[28]

In addition to fitting the stock stereotypes of Black dysfunction, Clinton also had a Black best friend and appeared genuinely comfortable around working-class Black people. All of this set him apart from other presidents and from White politicians in general. As an honorary Black person, Clinton received Black protectionism's highest vote count. Following the allegations and admissions that the married president had had sexual relations with a twenty-four-year-old White House intern,[29] poll data indicated that the majority of Blacks stood behind him.[30] At the end of Clinton's second term as president, surveys showed that he had the support of more than 80 percent of the Black community. Clinton's approval ratings peaked during his impeachment trial. The Black voting bloc consistently represented one of Clinton's strongest bases of support.

This well of Black support was again on display following Clinton's departure from the White House. After he faced heated criticism about his first choice in office space—a midtown Manhattan office that rented for almost $1 million annually—Clinton opted to move uptown, to Harlem.[31] On the heels of this, his grant of an executive pardon and clemency in several controversial cases was heavily criticized.[32] As before, Clinton's Black base remained steadfast. This support has taken many forms. It includes Clinton's induction into the Arkansas Black Hall of Fame in 2002. Of the sixty-two members, Clinton was its first and only White inductee.[33] In another symbolic indication of Blacks standing behind Clinton, in 2002 he was named honorary chairman of the Charleston, South Carolina, Museum of African American History.

Jesse Jackson

The Reverend Jesse Jackson has been an active civil rights leader for more than four decades. He has held a variety of posts, including a brief term as shadow-senator in the District of Columbia,[34] peacekeeper, presidential advisor, hostage negotiator, presidential candidate, corporate-diversity broker, boycott leader, and head of Rainbow/PUSH and the Citizenship Education Fund (CEF). In January 2001, Jackson, who is the married father of five, admitted fathering a child with his mistress.[35] The story, which first appeared in the *National Enquirer*, was widely reported by the tabloids and mainstream press.[36] The mother of Jackson's two-year-old love child, Karin Stanford, had been a Rainbow/PUSH consultant and had authored a biography of Jackson.[37]

The Jackson story ignited intense media interest. Jackson held press conferences to respond to the charges.[38] Based upon information that was subsequently released, the CEF's financial management became an issue. As well, Stanford's receipt of $40,000—to move from Washington, D.C., to California—was criticized.[39] During this period, Jackson maintained a high public profile within the Black community, including a well-timed, very late arrival to a nationally televised panel on the "State of Black America," hosted by Tavis Smiley. The crowd gave him a rousing, minutes-long, standing ovation. Polls indicate that support for Jackson remained strong within the Black community.[40] This allegiance may be partly attributable to the timing of the press reports. On January 20, 2001, Jackson was scheduled to lead a national rally in Tallahassee, Florida.[41] The march was designed to draw attention to the 2000 Florida election scandal and to protest the presidential inauguration of George W. Bush.[42] Two days before the scheduled forum, the Jackson story broke.

In the year 2000, there was a noteworthy alliance between Reynolds, Clinton, and Jackson. Reynolds, who had served three years of his sentence, was released in 2000, following a commutation by Bill Clinton.[43] Jackson's Rainbow/PUSH organization subsequently hired Reynolds as a consultant on prison reform.[44]

John Street

On October 7, 2003, wiretap devices were found in the office of Philadelphia's mayor, John Street.[45] At this time, Street, a Democrat, was waging a reelection campaign against Tom Katz, a Republican. The Philadelphia police discovered the wiretaps while conducting a routine electronic sweep of the mayor's city hall office. Because the FBI was tight-lipped about the cause of the investigation, it was initially unclear whether Street, who is African American, was the target of the probe. After almost two weeks of citywide speculation, a federal official indicated that Mayor Street was not the central focus of the search.[46] Specifically, the federal authorities were investigating municipal contracts.[47] The FBI stated that no incriminating evidence against Street was found in the undercover investigation.[48]

In addition to the concerns raised about the wiretapping, the tactics used by Street's rival were also questioned by African Americans.[49] Approximately one week prior to the election, African American support for the Philadelphia mayor rose from 70 percent to 84 percent.[50] Street won reelection by a 60 percent to 40 percent margin.

Notably, Street himself sounded the call for Black protectionism. He suggested that the FBI investigation was part of a racially motivated plot to take down the African American mayor of a large city.[51] Discussing the wiretaps, Street commented, "There are some people, particularly in the African American community, who believe that this is too much of a coincidence to be a coincidence."[52]

Based on the above discussion, it appears that Black protectionism is readily granted to politicians. Each of the politicians, all men, benefited to some degree from racial protectionism. One explanation for this groundswell of "Black love" could be the nature of the charges leveled against politicians. In three of the five cases, the offenses were what some call "victimless" crimes—that is, adultery and drug use. The next section addresses whether Black protectionism applies to Black women.

Black Women

Is Black protectionism solely the province of Black men? Only a handful of Black women have been eligible for Black protectionism. Only one has received it. The fact that so few Black women have been eligible for its protection may simply reflect national trends, indicating that women, compared with men, have relatively low rates of involvement in the criminal justice system. What follows is a discussion of seven Black women who were potential recipients of Black protectionism. Four are politicians, political appointees, or potential appointees, Carol Moseley-Braun, Alexis Herman, Lani Guinier, and Joycelyn Elders, and three are entertainers, Lisa Lopes, Diana Ross, and Janet Jackson.[53]

Carol Moseley-Braun

In 1992, Moseley-Braun became the first Black woman to be elected to the U.S. senate. During her tenure, she faced allegations that she had used campaign funds for personal expenses and ignored claims that her campaign manager was mishandling affairs, and she was criticized for maintaining an alliance with Nigerian dictator Sani Abacha.[54] Ultimately, there was no finding of criminal wrongdoing against Moseley-Braun.[55] Ironically, Moseley-Braun, elected in the aftermath of the Clarence Thomas hearings, did not benefit from the same protectionism he received. In 1998, she lost her reelection bid, in 1999 she was appointed U.S. ambassador to Samoa and New Zealand, and in 2004 she ran as a presidential candidate in the Democratic primaries.

Alexis Herman

In 1998, Alexis Herman, the secretary of labor, faced allegations of bribery. Specifically, she was accused of having accepted $250,000 in illegal campaign contributions.[56] A special prosecutor was appointed and following a two-year investigation, Herman was cleared of all charges.[57] As was the case for Moseley-Braun, the Black community appeared to take little notice of these charges—not enough to cause pollsters to track their reactions.

Lani Guinier and Joycelyn Elders

The incidents involving Lani Guinier and Joycelyn Elders are different from those involving Moseley-Braun and Herman. Neither Guinier's nor Elders's case involved a charge of criminal or unethical conduct (see table 3.1). Their cases are noteworthy, however, because at the time they were accused of wrongdoing, they were either in or nominated for high-profile posts.

In 1993, Bill Clinton nominated Guinier to head the civil rights division of the United States Attorney General's office. Conservatives rallied in opposition. Guinier, then a University of Pennsylvania law professor, was portrayed as a left-wing kook—a quota queen with "a strange name, strange hair, and strange writings."[58] On the brink of her confirmation hearing, before she could respond to her critics, Clinton withdrew her name.[59] He said that after reviewing her legal scholarship he could no longer support her nomination.[60] There was very little public response from the Black community. Perhaps because the controversy involved legal writing and because Guinier was accused not of a crime, but rather "inappropriate" writings, support for her was less than forthcoming. Guinier observes, however, that she received behind the scenes support from Black politicians and grass roots community members. Guinier, who now teaches at Harvard, is the first woman of color to receive tenure at the law school.

Similarly, Joycelyn Elders's forced resignation from her post as U.S. surgeon general did little to spark Black interest. Elders served as surgeon general from 1993 to 1994.[61] During her tenure, she made several frank remarks indicating her support for needle exchange programs, equal access to abortion, and the legalization of drugs.[62] It was Elders's comments on sex education in grade school, however, that resulted in her dismissal. In December 1994, Elders spoke at the United Nations on World AIDS day. In response to a psychologist's question about whether she would recommend masturbation to discourage school children from riskier forms of sexual activity, Elders stated, "I think that it is something that is a part of human sexuality and a part of something that perhaps should be taught."[63] A few days following her comments, Clinton asked for Elder's resignation—stating that she held values "contrary to the administration."[64]

There was relatively little comment within the Black community regarding these four cases. This is especially noteworthy in Herman's case since she was charged with serious criminal conduct. Also, it is ironic that Elders received little vocal support from the African American community, considering that her work has focused on reducing the Black community's high rate of sexually transmitted diseases, particularly HIV/AIDS. Neither the Guinier nor Elders cases involved a charge of misconduct—a common trigger for Black protectionism. This may explain why both cases fell below the Black community's radar. In fact, no national poll information was found on the general public's reaction to any of these controversies. The muted community response to these four cases may be explained by the fact that they were each viewed as a low stakes political scandal.

Regarding Guinier and Elders, it is also possible that their cases involved a test of competing allegiances. Clinton, who arguably is viewed as an honorary Black person by many African Americans, was the person directly responsible for denying Guinier a confirmation hearing and asking for Elders's resignation. It may be that when forced to choose, Blacks extend the hand of protectionism to the person seen as having the most racial seniority or the most power. The fact that many people are uncomfortable discussing sex, especially masturbation, no doubt affected the amount of public support for Elders.

Lisa "Left Eye" Lopes

In 1994, Lisa Lopes, one-third of the hip-hop girl group, TLC, burned down the home she shared with Atlanta Falcons football player Andre Rison. Lopes, in an alcohol-fueled rage, following an argument with Rison, started a fire in the bathtub. The fire quickly spread to the rest of the 1.3 million dollar mansion, burning it down. Lopes pled guilty to first-degree arson and was sentenced to a halfway house and five years' probation, and fined $10,000. She was also ordered to undergo alcoholic rehabilitation for twenty-eight days.

Lopes's case has several noteworthy dimensions. Most strikingly, it is the only Black protectionism case that involves a Black woman charged with a serious, street crime felony offense. The person victimized in the case, Rison, is an African American man. It is not surprising that the case drew lots of media coverage. It involved two Black celebrities—Rison was a respected NFL player and Lopes was a member of one of the best-selling girl groups in music history. As well, the couple was known for its volatile on-again, off-again relationship.

While the case generated interest, speculation, and talk, it did not invoke Black protectionism. Many viewed the case as a private domestic squabble. Additionally, Lopes admitted to the crime and Rison stood by her side in court. In 2002, Lopes died in a car accident in Honduras.

Diana Ross

In December 2002, singing legend Diana Ross was charged with driving under the influence. Ross was arrested in Tucson, Arizona, after she was found driving her car southbound in a northbound lane. It was determined that Ross's blood alcohol level was .20, more than twice the permissible state level of .08. She pled no contest and served a forty-eight-hour jail sentence. In February 2004 she was sentenced to one year of unsupervised probation.

Ross's arrest and charge received a great deal of media attention. She was largely ridiculed by the press—made the butt of jokes on late-night television and used as tabloid fodder. Black media outlets did not staunchly defend Ross. Perhaps the fact that there was a videotape of Ross's arrest, along with her public persona as a difficult diva, partly explain the denial of protectionism in her case. However, the few sympathetic, nonjudgmental reactions to Ross's predicament appeared to come from Black media. For instance, in May 2004, *Essence* magazine did a cover feature of Ross and her daughter, actress Tracee Ellis Ross. The article, which focused on Ross as a mother, mentioned the drunk driving incident only in passing.

Janet Jackson

During the half-time show of the 2004 Super Bowl, Janet Jackson and Justin Timberlake sang "Rock Your Body"—a song that had been recorded by Timberlake. As the song concluded, Timberlake grabbed and pulled off the right side of Jackson's leather bustier—exposing her right breast, which was adorned with a nipple shield. This "exposure" came just as Timberlake was singing the lyrics, "I'll have you naked by the end of this song."

Needless to say, the event caused a media tempest. In the days that followed, Jackson was accused of sullying the Super Bowl (a mom-and-apple-pie tradition) and devising the performance "trick" to create interest in her soon-to-be released album, and she was generally blamed for the decline of morality in society. The Federal Communications Commission threatened fines, a class action lawsuit was filed to redress the harms resulting from Jackson's unexpected breast baring, and Jackson was uninvited to the Grammy Awards that were scheduled for the following week.

This case provides a rare opportunity to compare the treatment of a Black and White person involved in the same incident. Timberlake quickly distanced himself from the episode—referring to it as a "wardrobe malfunction." He said that he had no part in planning the incident and apologized to anyone who was offended. He stated that he and Jackson had agreed on a last-minute routine change—he was to pull down the right side of her bustier to reveal a red camisole. According to Timberlake, however, he did not know that the prearranged stunt would reveal Jackson's breast. After agreeing to apologize at the Grammy awards, Timberlake was allowed to participate.

In contrast, Jackson's video-recorded apology appeared to fall upon deaf ears. She stated that the "costume reveal" she had planned was not supposed to completely bare her breast. It is clear that Jackson was uninvited to the Grammy Awards ceremony; what is unclear, however, is whether she was reinvited as was Timberlake—either with or without stipulations—and declined to reapologize. Bottom line: Jackson was blamed and criticized for the entire incident.

Interestingly, Jackson received a good deal of support from the Black community. Other high-profile African Americans, including Chris Rock, recording artist Usher, and comedian Eddie Griffin, voiced their support for Jackson. When discussing the incident, Black media outlets, including Internet chat rooms (e.g., BET), magazines (e.g., *Ebony* magazine), and radio commentary (e.g., Tom Joyner), honed in on three aspects of the case. First, it appeared that Timberlake was being let off of the hook for his role in the incident. This was especially troubling, as some noted, because it was Timberlake's actions that resulted in the revealing of Jackson's breast. In a legal sense, he was the direct cause of the incident. Others commented that Timberlake's actions, wittingly or unwittingly, amounted to a violent visual portrayal of a White man ripping off a Black woman's clothing.

Second, some argued that Jackson was made the scapegoat for what was already a raunchy, non-family-friendly half-time show. In addition to the Jackson/Timberlake performance, the other half-time acts (e.g., Nelly) featured scantily clad women and men dancing in a sexually explicit manner (e.g., crotch-grabbing). Further, some of the Super Bowl commercials were themselves offensive. Add to all of this the overall spectacle of men wildly rushing into one another for sport.

Third, some suggested that the media focus on Janet Jackson was part of a larger plan to bring down the famous Jackson family. Fuel was added to this conspiracy theory when Jackson's brother Michael faced a second round of pedophilia charges during the same period as the Super Bowl incident. His new greatest hits CD, *Number Ones,* was due to be released the same week that the charges were filed (his case is discussed in the next section of this chapter).

In other signs of support, one month following the incident, Janet Jackson received a Soul Train music award (the Quincy Jones award for career achievement). During the spring of 2004, she was also featured on the covers of *Ebony* and *Essence* magazines. Jackson also received tacit support from some of the mainstream media. For instance, in April 2004 she was the guest host and musical guest on *Saturday Night Live.*

The Black community's embrace of Janet Jackson was extraordinary given that as a group, Black women do not appear to be eligible for Black protectionism. With the exception of Jackson, they leave the well of Black protectionism empty-handed. The fact that Jackson's treatment could be readily compared with that of a White entertainer in the same circumstances may have propelled the Black community's interest in the case.

With the exception of the Jackson case (and to some degree the Lopes case), the incidents involving Black women have generated little interest within the African American community. It is important to note, however, that Lopes's case is the only one that involved a street crime. While arson is a felony offense, the circumstances of the case (domestic dispute) may have made it even less likely that community members would pass judgment. Unlike the cases involving Black men, none of these involve murder or sexual assault. In fact, two of the cases (Guinier and Elders) did not involve an allegation of criminal offense. While Black protectionism appears unavailable to Black women who find themselves accused of crime or "inappropriate" behavior, it remains to be seen how a well-known Black woman accused of murder or sexual assault would fare—a scenario that would test the gender dimension of Black protectionism. The Black community's response in the above cases may have been muted precisely because the stakes were perceived as relatively low, when compared with the cases involving Black men. Thus, assessing the availability of protectionism for Black women is difficult because the community has remained mostly silent in these cases.

Sexual Assault Cases[65]

Each of the cases discussed in this section involves a high-profile African American man who was charged with sexual assault or sexual harassment. The group includes a justice (Clarence Thomas), athletes (Mike Tyson and Kobe Bryant), and entertainers (R. Kelly and Michael Jackson). With the exception of one case where there was a videotape, the cases came down to "She said/He said."

Clarence Thomas

In July 1991, President George H. W. Bush nominated Clarence Thomas to fill the vacancy on the U.S. Supreme Court created by Justice Thurgood Marshall's retirement.[66] Questions were raised within the civil rights and Black communities as to whether Thomas was a worthy choice to succeed Marshall, the first African American Supreme Court Justice. The Black political community was split in its response to the Thomas nomination. The NAACP waited one month before issuing a statement, saying that it was "with regret" that the organization could not support Thomas.[67] Notably, the NAACP's Legal Defense Fund opposed the nomination. The Congressional Black Caucus, in a symbolic action, voted 19 to 1 against the nomination.[68] In contrast, the Urban League[69] and the Nation of Islam offered support for Thomas.[70]

Among the Black grassroots, however, the Thomas nomination continued to gain momentum.[71] Support for Thomas rose dramatically once Anita Hill's claim of sexual harassment was made public.[72] In September 1991, the press learned of her disclosures to the FBI during its background check on Thomas. Hill, who had worked for Thomas twelve years earlier, alleged that Thomas had routinely subjected her to crude, sexually explicit remarks and lewd behaviors. Hill was portrayed as a scorned woman, a woman in search of her fifteen minutes of fame on the back of a Black man, a wild-eyed feminist pawn of the National Organization for Women, a deranged woman suffering from "erotomania" (a rare clinical disease that describes someone who has delusional sexual fantasies), and as a Black woman who was angry that her ex-lover, Thomas, had chosen to marry a White woman.[73] In October 1991, Thomas's nomination to the Supreme Court was confirmed in a 52 to 48 Senate vote.[74]

Mike Tyson

In 1992, Mike Tyson was charged with sexually assaulting Desiree Washington, an eighteen-year-old college student.[75] Tyson met Washington in Ohio, during rehearsals for the Miss Black America beauty pageant. Washington was a contestant, Tyson a judge. Tyson called her later that evening and they agreed to meet. Washington went to Tyson's hotel room after midnight and according to Washington, he raped her. Tyson, who steadfastly denied the charges, was convicted of rape and served three years in prison.[76]

From the time the charges were made public, the Black community roundly denounced Washington. She was either blamed for her extreme naïveté (e.g., "What, besides sex, would a grown man want from a woman in the middle of the night?") or labeled a scheming gold-digger, who planned to lure the boxing champ into a sexual encounter, have sex, "cry rape," and then cash in.[77] Washington's assertions that she had no ulterior motives and that she was thrilled to meet Tyson (one of her father's sports heroes) were dismissed as self-serving.

As the trigger questions predict (table 3.3, questions 3, 5, and 7), many Blacks concluded that Tyson faced a double standard. For instance, during the same period that Tyson faced rape charges, William Kennedy Smith was acquitted of rape. Smith, the nephew of President John F. Kennedy, to the manor born, and White, stood in stark contrast to Tyson, who had no elite pedigree, was Black, and was convicted of rape. When Tyson was released from prison, there was a welcome home parade held for him in Harlem. Event organizers included boxing promoter Don King, Congressman Charles Rangel, community activist Al Sharpton, and singer Roberta Flack. Some African Americans staged a counterprotest.[78]

Tyson's rape conviction made headlines again ten years later. In a 2004 interview, Tyson stated that if given the chance today he would rape

Desiree Washington and her mother. He blames them for his conviction, which he says led to the demise of his boxing career and caused other personal problems.

In both the Clarence Thomas and Mike Tyson cases, the Black female accuser was not as well known as the Black man. Until the allegations surfaced, most people had not heard of either Hill or Washington. These women could not avail themselves of Black protectionism since neither woman had a "national reputation." Further, neither one had credibility as a racial spokesperson. Notably, outside of legal circles, Thomas was not well-known at the time he was nominated to the Supreme Court. By the time Hill's allegations surfaced one month later, however, Thomas had a "national reputation," sufficient to initiate Black protectionism.

R. Kelly

The child pornography case involving rhythm and blues crooner R. Kelly raises some important insights into the workings of Black protectionism. In 2002, Kelly faced a twenty-one-count criminal indictment by the Chicago prosecutor's office.[79] One of the allegations was second-degree rape—specifically, engaging in sexual intercourse with a girl under the age of fourteen. Kelly, then a thirty-four-year-old married father of three, denied the charges.[80] The crown jewel of the prosecution's case was a graphic thirty-minute videotape of the alleged unlawful sexual activity. Underground copies of the video were sold on the street and circulated over the Internet.

The public's response to pornography charges against Kelly has been mixed. More than in other cases eligible for Black protectionism, people seem to want to separate their feelings about R. Kelly, the man, from their feelings about R. Kelly, the musician. Very few (beyond Kelly's inner circle) have publicly suggested that he was innocent or that he was set up (table 3.3, question 2). There was no evidence that the government was "out to get him." Instead, one thread of the public reaction and commentary has focused on Kelly's talent as singer and songwriter, noting that what he does in his private life should remain private. Another thread has focused on the young girl's actions, such as comments that she was "fast" or questions about her parents ("Where were they?").

This perspective helps explain how Kelly's 2003 CD release, *Chocolate Factory*, which debuted at first place on the Billboard charts,[81] went on to reach double platinum status (selling more than two million copies). It was also nominated for several music awards, including a Grammy Award, Soul Train Music Award, and an NAACP Image Award. Kelly received a Soul Train Music award, named for Quincy Jones, for career achievement. In June 2004, he was featured on the cover of *Vibe* magazine.

On the flip side, Kelly has received little vocal support. For instance, there has been no queue of celebrities standing up to publicly defend Kelly. Further, his nomination for an NAACP award drew outrage. Many took issue with the idea that he might be eligible to win an "image" award—traditionally viewed as an accolade reserved for upstanding Blacks. The criticism leveled against the NAACP was so harsh that the leadership removed the nominations process from its general membership and imposed a "morals clause" for future nominees.

Further, Kelly does not appear to have a public reservoir of goodwill. It is likely that what little the public knew about his personal life did not work in his favor. When Kelly was twenty-five, he married then-fifteen-year-old singer Aaliyah. Also, throughout his career Kelly has faced allegations that he engaged in sex with underage girls.[82] And his lust-laden lyrics themselves lend tacit support to the sex-related charges. Unlike the Marion Barry case, the existence of a videotape worked against Kelly. The video allowed everyone to observe, in graphic detail, Kelly's sexual liaison with a minor. Further, the offense of pedophilia is viewed as a more serious crime than consensual drug use.

Kobe Bryant

In July 2003, NBA superstar Kobe Bryant was charged with sexual assault. Bryant, who is Black, was accused of raping a nineteen-year-old White hotel clerk, in Eagle County, Colorado. After initially denying any sexual contact with the woman, Bryant, who is married, admitted to having a sexual encounter, saying it was consensual. Bryant, who at the time was a beloved athlete, benefited from his image as a clean-cut family man.

Shortly after he was charged, Bryant and his wife attended the Teen Choice Awards, where he won for favorite male athlete. In his acceptance speech, Bryant, who wore a T-shirt with a picture of Muhammad Ali, stated "An injustice anywhere is an injustice everywhere." This represents a slight rewording of Martin Luther King Jr.'s famous statement, "Injustice anywhere is a threat to justice everywhere." Bryant's comments were surprising given that throughout his career he has rarely spoken publicly about race or politics. Many dismissed them as a self-serving attempt to jump-start the Black community's support.

Although both Blacks and Whites have voiced support for Bryant, the Black community's support has been strongest. An August 2003 poll reported that two-thirds of the Blacks surveyed said they were "very" or "somewhat" sympathetic toward Bryant.[83] This compares with 40 percent of the Whites who participated in the survey. Both historical and case-related facts put the issue of race at the fore.[84] Some observers, for instance, point to the history of false rape charges made against Black men by White women (e.g., the Scottsboro Boys case and the Rosewood massacre)[85] and have suggested that Bryant was "set up."[86]

Adding to this mix, during the case the National Alliance, a White supremacist group, distributed fliers warning, "Don't have sex with blacks."[87] The Eagle County sheriff's department ordered "anti-Kobe" T-shirts, including one style that featured a small hangman on the front, and on the back, Bryant's jersey number. The shirt read, "I'm not a rapist: I'm just a cheater."[88] Bryant played in the 2003–2004 basketball season to crowd cheers and jeers. In January 2004, McDonald's declined to renew Bryant's endorsement contract. In May 2004, Bryant pled not guilty to the rape charges. In September 2004, the rape charges were dropped after the victim declined to testify at the trial. Bryant has since faced declining popularity. This occurred in part because many were put off by the charges and by Bryant's belated reluctant admission that he had an adulterous relationship, and many believe he was largely responsible for the Lakers team's trade of his teammate, Shaquille O'Neal, and the nonrenewal of coach Phil Jackson's contract.

Michael Jackson

In November 2003 Michael Jackson's home was raided. Pursuant to a search warrant, seventy-plus officers from the Santa Barbara Sheriff's Office carried out the unannounced search of Jackson's Neverland ranch. Within a few days Jackson, who had been out of town, returned home. He was arrested and bail was set at $3 million. The forty-five-year-old star was charged with multiple counts of child molestation. His criminal trial began in March 2005. Ten years earlier, Jackson had faced similar allegations.[89]

Jackson and his family denied the charges and claimed they were part of an extortion-revenge plot. In an interview with Barbara Walters, Michael's older brother Jermaine Jackson was adamant that race played a role in the prosecutor's decision to file charges: "They're a bunch of racist rednecks out there who don't care about people."[90] He also stressed that the charges have to be considered within the context of America's historically racist treatment of Blacks. An example of this racially disparate treatment is the difference between Jackson's case and Phil Spector's case. Spector, a renowned record producer, is White. In 2003, when he was charged with murder, his bail was set at $1 million. By contrast, the bail set for Jackson, who was charged with sexual assault, was $3 million.

Over the course of the case, the Black community's support for Jackson has ebbed and flowed.[91] A December 2003 poll indicated that 54 percent of Blacks had a "favorable" opinion of Jackson, compared with 14 percent of Whites.[92] Black support mounted in his case as the prosecutors delayed filing formal charges against Jackson. As well, a February 2004 report by the Children and Family Services office indicated that child abuse charges were unfounded.[93] In January 2005, on the eve of jury selection in his trial, Jackson released a statement. Jackson said, "Let me have my day in court. I deserve a fair trial like every other American citizen. I love my community and have great faith in our justice system."[94] Jackson's vague reference to "my community," could be interpreted as the African American community. During the trial, Jackson's appeal to the Black community was more direct. In an interview with Jesse Jackson, Michael Jackson compared himself with Nelson Mandela, Jack Johnson, and Muhammad Ali, stating that like them, he had been unjustly accused of wrongdoing.

Throughout the case, questions surfaced about Jackson's "Blackness." Some asked whether Jackson is entitled to claim Blackness given both his extensive plastic surgery (to alter what had been the face and body of a handsome young Black man) and his mostly White inner circle. Some Whites have also raised issues about Jackson's racial authenticity. For example, MSNBC cable-TV host Chris Matthews asked whether Jackson could be considered "Black" given his physical transformation. Connie Rice, a Black Los Angeles attorney, suggests that in order for race to come into play, "The case has to involve society's powerful taboos, and that essentially means it has to involve a virile black male." Rice notes that the issue of race in the Jackson case is complicated because he no longer looks Black and he also has an androgynous appearance.

It is clear that the Black community has a special affinity for Michael Jackson. Many have grown up with Jackson or watched him grow up. They remember him and his brothers singing and dancing—providing the soul music sound track for the 1970s and 1980s. In his 2004 "Never Scared" tour, Chris Rock, commenting on this strong allegiance, joked that Blacks love Michael Jackson so much that they gave him a "pass" in the first child abuse case.

Some of Black protectionism's strongest showings have occurred in the context of sexual assault cases. The Black community is particularly resolute in defending Black men accused of rape or assault. The protective embrace is strongest when the victim is White. This is directly linked to the history of false allegations of rape by White women claiming they were assaulted by Black men.

Athletes and Rappers

Athletes

Those with athletic prowess enjoy an exalted place in the heart of the Black community. Black athletes were among the first to break the color barrier. They were living proof that Blackness did not equal inferiority. They became "credits to the race." Within the community, athletes were among the first to achieve the American dream. All of this success was achieved in the face of virulent racism. During the period of legalized racial segregation, Black sportsmen were dismissed and denigrated as physically unfit to compete against Whites. Prior to the 1960s, professional Black athletes faced segregation on and off of the playing field (see chapter 1).

The way the Black community has responded to athletes in trouble presents a long-standing and complex application of Black protectionism. In recent years, there have been numerous criminal cases involving Black athletes. Few, however, have sparked national interest and a closing of Black ranks. As detailed above, only a handful of athletes, such as O.J. Simpson, Kobe Bryant, and Mike Tyson, have received the protective Black shield. Most other cases elicited little more than a shrug. It may be that people have low expectations for Black athletes.

One case that received a good deal of attention involved NBA player Latrell Sprewell. In 1997, Sprewell, who then played for the Golden State Warriors, was charged with choking his coach, P. J. Carlesimo. A videotape of the encounter showed Sprewell's hands around Carlesimo's neck. The mainstream media came down hard on Sprewell. He instantly became the poster child for all of the excesses and failures of young professional athletes. In the middle of this heated controversy, San Francisco's mayor Willie Brown, who is African American, poured oil on the fire. He commented, "His boss may have needed choking. It may have been justified . . . someone should have asked the question, 'What prompted that?'"[95] These remarks set off additional rounds of comment and dissent. Brown's remarks reflect a special form of Black protectionism—cases in which another well-known Black comes to the aid of a prominent Black who faces legal troubles. Brown sought to highlight the fact that several other players had problems with Carlesimo. These comments, however, were largely ignored. Ultimately, the NBA decided to suspend Sprewell for one year.

In several cases involving Black athletes, the Black community's response has been muted (e.g., Ray Lewis) and in some instances the response has been scornful (e.g., Rae Carruth and Jayson Williams). In many incidents involving athletes, Black protectionism has not been the knee-jerk response; instead, the community has taken a wait-and-see approach. These responses suggest that Black protectionism is available on a restricted basis for athletes.

Rappers

It is not only athletes who have limited access to the cloak of racial protectionism. It does not appear to be readily available to rappers either. Many of the rappers who have been charged with criminal offences are not eligible for Black protectionism. First, very few rappers have achieved national recognition, a requirement for Black protectionism. Second, there appears to be a class bias with Black protectionism. This is a twist since many of the rappers who are eligible for protectionism are rich but do not adhere to the mainstream image of what rich looks like. This may reflect a generational bias in Black protectionism (e.g., that older Blacks are more likely to receive it).

Sean "P. Diddy" Combs presents an interesting case, in that he is more than a rapper. Combs, who owns a music label, clothing line, and restaurant chain, is an actor, and donates large sums of money to charity, could be said to transcend the rapper label. During his 1999 trial for weapons possession, Combs received a mixed response from the Black community. Some argued that he had built his professional career on a "gangsta" image and was now paying the price for it. Others believed that he had been targeted for the same reasons as O.J. Simpson—because he was a successful and famous Black man.

Second, for various reasons, it appears that many people have low expectations for rappers: It is not surprising when they get into legal trouble. Adding to this, many rappers have spent time behind bars and have used these experiences as material for their recordings. For some, the authenticity of rappers hinges on their "street credibility"—which is enhanced by serving jail time. Further, many people link rap music with crime.[96]

All told, the Black community appears less concerned when a rapper is charged with criminal conduct than when other celebrity members face charges. Some segments within the Black community, notably young fans of hip-hop music, however, are likely to rally behind rappers.

Bill Cosby: A Special Note

Bill Cosby is an internationally revered and widely loved entertainer. Over the years he has faced several allegations of adultery and sexual assault. While Cosby has admitted to having an extramarital affair, he has denied fathering a child, Autumn Jackson, out of wedlock. He has also denied allegations of sexual assault.

In May 2004, Cosby made several controversial remarks at an NAACP event celebrating the fiftieth anniversary of the U.S. Supreme Court's *Brown v. Board of Education* decision. In his remarks, Cosby was harshly critical of poor Blacks. Among his comments, he said, "[T]he lower economic people are not holding up their end of this deal. . . . These people are not parenting. They are buying things for their kids—$500 sneakers for what? And won't spend $200 for 'Hooked on Phonics.' . . . They're standing on the corner and can't speak English."[97]

Cosby's remarks polarized many within the African American community. Many stepped forward to criticize Cosby, taking issue with his message, criticizing it for what was left out, assailing it as incoherent, or questioning the forum wherein he delivered his remarks.[98] Others saw

Cosby as properly airing dirty laundry. Following the groundswell of criticism, Cosby stood by and reiterated his opinions.

Cosby's case is special for several reasons. First, because of his status as an African American elder who has arguably paid his race dues. Second, his philanthropic work is legendary. Cosby and his wife, Camille, have donated millions of dollars to Black colleges (including Howard University and Spelman College).

Third, the issues he raised are subject to a long-standing debate within the African American community. In this way, then, the incident does not involve a charge or allegation of wrongdoing by the state or federal government. Cosby's remarks test the limits of Black protectionism. Specifically, they raise the issue of whether the Black community will protect prominent Blacks who are publicly *critical* of other, poor, African Americans.

Conclusion

This chapter provides a comprehensive overview of how Black protectionism works. The emerging picture shows that Black protectionism is a wide-ranging, dynamic phenomenon. Its availability and application suggest some themes. First, it is almost always triggered to shield Black men. There is only one instance of its successful application to a Black woman. Second, the onset of protectionism is affected by how the famous Black person is treated by the media. Protectionism acts as a stopgap to avoid "piling on." Once the media begins to circle its wagons around a well-known Black man, protectionism works to mitigate or dismiss the allegations. Third, protectionism embraces Blacks who come from a wide variety of political backgrounds—conservative, liberal, and where one's politics are unknown. Many recipients, however, are tied to the civil rights community. Fourth, the degree of seriousness of the allegation does not appear to determine the availability of Black protectionism. It has been applied in cases involving murder, rape, and child sexual abuse. Based on the discussion of how Black protectionism is currently applied, the next chapter examines how Black community members perceive and apply Black protectionism. They address not only how it works, but also, how it might work more effectively.

© Geri Engberg/The Image Works

CHAPTER FOUR

TALKING COMMUNITY

Whenever a Black person's in trouble, as a knee-jerk reaction, I always
say, "They're not guilty."

—Dave Chappelle, comedian

Introduction

In the statement quoted above, David Chappelle identifies his own practice of Black protectionism. He continues:

> The premise of reasonable doubt for a Black person and for a White person are two separate things. For a White person, the idea that the police planted evidence is ridiculous: "The police are here to serve and protect us!" Yeah *you*. But to a Black person, it's not ridiculous. The FBI followed Martin Luther King around! Was he a threat to America?[1]

Chappelle is not alone. Many Blacks believe that there are two justice systems, one for Whites and another one for everyone else. The perception that there is a racial double standard of treatment extends beyond the criminal justice system to include how Blacks are treated within U.S. social institutions, including the media. Contemporary media stories provide strong support for this perspective.

The 2003 news story involving U.S. soldier Jessica Lynch offers a case in point. Lynch, a soldier in the U.S. war on Iraq, received an unprecedented amount of press attention following an injury. The media focus on her provides an interesting contrast with the attention received by her unit-mate Shoshanna Johnson. Both women, one White, one Black, were seriously injured during their tour. Lynch suffered severe leg injuries when her vehicle turned over. Johnson, who was a POW for three weeks, suffered severe injuries after being shot through both of her ankles. Johnson's injuries prevented her from standing for long periods of time. Although Lynch consistently said she was not a war hero, the press heralded her as one. In addition to having her biography published, her story was featured in a made-for-TV movie, she appeared on the cover of *Time* magazine, and she was interviewed on numerous television shows, including *The Today Show* and *Late Night with David Letterman*. Following her discharge from the army, Lynch was granted an 80 percent disability benefit. In contrast, upon retirement, Johnson received 30 percent of her disability benefit. The press was a Johnny-come-lately to Shoshanna Johnson's story. Many believe that the difference in press interest and coverage was a matter of Black and White.[2]

Comparing cases such as those of Lynch and Johnson provides insight into the climate in which Black protectionism operates. This chapter builds and expands on the previous one, which reviewed how protectionism works to shield Black celebrities. By presenting the voices of everyday Black people, it adds further insight into the how and why of Black protectionism. The discussion is based on an analysis of focus group interviews with African Americans.

Voices from the Community

Thus far, most of the discussion and analysis of the Black community's perspective on and application of Black protectionism has relied on media reports, polls, and surveys. The findings of three focus groups, with a total of thirty Blacks, who range in age from eighteen to seventy years old,[3] incorporate the voices of average, nonfamous community members into the discussion. The majority of participants in the first two group interviews were under age thirty. A third focus group was held to gather a wider age range of respondents and perspectives. Most of the participants were born in the United States and most were women. All three focus group interviews were held in November and December 2004. The discussion was designed to get community members to talk about the application of Black protectionism to

Black celebrities. Specifically, the interviews were structured to invite participants to consider why protectionism exists; how it works; its value and cost; and what changes, if any, might make it work more effectively.

Do We Need Black Protectionism?

Not only did most participants agree that Blacks tend to protect their own, they also agreed on the reasons for protectionism. Their rationales can be placed into two overlapping categories: First, that celebrities are proxies for Blacks as a group and second, that the history of American racism, including government conspiracies to bring Blacks down, makes Black protectionism necessary.

Jasmine, a twenty-one-year-old college student, commented, "[Celebrities] represent us as Black people because each of us wants to be successful. . . . If someone makes it big and they find a way to catch him up (charge him with a crime) it will take away from us." These sentiments were echoed by several participants, including Malik, a forty-eight-year-old community advocate. He offers an interesting twist on why celebrities such as O.J. Simpson are stand-ins for the Black community at large:

> We expect the Black male to be under attack. However, O.J. was . . . a bellwether for a lot of people. [Even though] he just "happened to be Black," he embodied what can happen to Black folks.

Jermaine, a twenty-one-year-old student from Jamaica, offered a similar take on the role of celebrities in symbolizing Black life:

> We see the celebrity as a Black person who has made it through oppression. We see that person as an icon for the Black community. So, we try to support the icon. If they go down, it's seen as another loss, another Black man has failed and has lost to the White man, once again.

Singling out those who are famous and popular for special protection is also an acknowledgment of the social odds of grand-scale success. Most Blacks, indeed most people, will not become rich and famous. Michelle, a twenty-one-year-old college student, insightfully observes that Black celebrities have "surreal lives . . . the chances of you having the things that they have are none." This perspective is fertile ground for Black protectionism. It underscores that rich and successful Blacks have a higher status and, thus, are entitled to differential treatment when they get into legal trouble.

In discussing how celebrities represent members of the Black community, several people mentioned the media's role in lumping Blacks together. Referring to the Kobe Bryant rape case, one participant stated that the media racializes Blacks' viewpoints—that it does not show Blacks as having diverse opinions about particular cases. Christina, a twenty-one-year-old student, says:

> [According to the media] whether or not I feel that Kobe was innocent or guilty is not because I feel that he was innocent or guilty, it is because I am Black and I feel that he is innocent because he's Black.

Jasmine agrees. She believes that Whites look at Blacks as a single entity: "They don't realize that we're unique. We come in all shades, shapes, and varieties. They look at us as a uniform group of people." In the focus group discussions, many used the Simpson case to support this viewpoint. For instance, during the Simpson trial, the media focused almost exclusively on the 70 percent of Blacks who believed he was innocent. This created the impression that the Black community is monolithic—thereby allowing the 70 percent to "speak" for 100 percent of the community.

There is a dynamic, reciprocal relationship between the media images of the Black community and the exercise of Black protectionism. When the media paints African Americans, particularly those who are famous, with a broad brush (e.g., as criminals and deviants), then Blacks respond in a common voice, by rejecting this negative characterization. In turn, this leads community members to further uphold celebrities as racial representatives, and this results in the community's defense of fallen Black entertainers and leaders, or icons. The cycle then repeats itself.

The history of racism in America was another theme that emerged to explain the presence of Black protectionism. Alicia, a thirty-nine-year-old office manager, described her mixed feelings based on the history of U.S. race relations:

> As a Black American, I have love and hate for this country. In the Constitution, we're the only ones who didn't count as people, we weren't men. It's unique to be in a country that wants you to fight for them and then they treat you like a second-class citizen. [Based on this history] it makes

sense to rally behind our Black celebrities. It's just a guise that we keep falling under, that we're all created equal.

In discussing the history of Black oppression, several shared their belief that there is an overall conspiracy to bring down African Americans, particularly those who have made it. The Scottsboro Boys and Emmett Till were cited by different participants as examples of Blacks whose cases were mishandled by the justice system. Referring to Michael Jackson and Kobe Bryant, Ebony, fifty-two, sighs:

> They need to leave them alone. I feel like there is just not justice out there for them. People are picking on them to see how much money they can get out of them. . . . I don't want to say it's racist, but I kind of feel like that.

Jasmine concurs, "You're never safe, and you never will make it because whether you have money or not, you will be targeted." This perspective ties in with another view that was offered—not only do Blacks have to work twice as hard to get ahead, they also have to be twice as careful not to get snagged by the criminal justice system.

We're Not Alone

In conversations about the existence of protectionism, several participants commented that Blacks have to look out for one another. Carmen, nineteen, asks, "If we don't support our own Black people, then who's going to support us?" At the same time that many participants said that Blacks should look out for other Blacks, many also said that other groups also protect their own—that individuals tend to look out for people who share their same characteristics. This is true not only for racial groups, but for groups in general. Kenny, a twenty-four-year-old graduate student, offered the following:

> If we examine other cultural and racial groups in the U.S., we see a lot of them pull together to help their people. Take for instance the Cubans in Miami. They have an ethnic enclave where they send for their people, employ their people, bring them over, and establish an entire community for themselves and build up wealth for themselves.

Related to this, it was also noted that there is within-group protectionism. Specifically, that African Americans protect their own in subgroups, including those who were born in the United States, those who are from the islands, and those who are from Africa. While noting that other racial groups guard members within their group, a few participants said American racism has bred a unique form of protectionism for Blacks. Charles, fifty, observes, "Certainly other ethnic groups have protectionism . . . [however,] we have it because of what has happened to us in the past."

Never Too Much?

The topic that generated the most heated debate and divergence of opinion during the focus group discussions was when Black protectionism should apply. At one end of the spectrum, a handful of participants argued that Black protectionism should always be available to Blacks—saying that there should be no restrictions.

Kenny boldly states, "I think Black protectionism should operate in all circumstances." Tony, a twenty-two-year-old student, shares this perspective. He comments, "I'm all about protecting each other, whenever, whatever, all the time, no matter what the situation is. . . . It's all about race." Both young men answered "yes," when asked whether they would apply protectionism even if they knew the person was guilty of a crime. Tony elaborates:

> Even if they did wrong, I feel that there's just something about rallying behind your own people. That's important to me. . . . So, yea, even if they're proven guilty.

This "no holds barred" protectionism stance raised the hackles of several members of the group who argued that protectionism should not be treated like a gift but rather something that is earned. Veronica, a thirty-eight-year-old psychologist, responds:

> To say that Black protectionism should apply across the board in any situation, no matter how horrific, is actually doing ourselves as a race, an injustice.

Further discussions, however, revealed another twist. At its core, the argument made by Kenny and Tony is that Black protectionism should operate as demand for procedural justice. Kenny explains, "We should protect them [to ensure] that they are given a proper trial and proper hearing in our court system." Focus group participants consistently agreed that anyone who is accused of a crime is entitled to have their constitutional rights protected; more to the point, that the Black community should stand up and assert these rights for celebrities and regular Black folks who find themselves in legal trouble. A few participants pointed out that the presumption of innocence means that we leave the determination of guilt to the justice system—not the media.

The issue of accountability also came up during the discussions. A few stressed that while the African American community should uphold the rights of other Blacks who have been accused of crime, the community should also hold them accountable. Carmen observes:

> A lot of times celebrities are glorified and put on a pedestal. This sends a message that it's okay if you raped someone and got away with it. It encourages athletes to think that they can get away with crime. It's important for people to realize, especially in the larger community, that right is right and wrong is wrong. If the person did it, they need to be held accountable. We need to show that as a Black community we support our people, but we also hold them accountable when they are guilty of crimes.

Focus group members did not provide details on how to hold famous Blacks accountable for wrongdoing. One person said that wrongdoers should no longer be treated as role models. At the same time, however, the same person observed that people in the limelight are already role models, whether we want them to be or not.

And the Victims?

During the discussions, several people asked about how Black protectionism treats Black victims of crime. A few expressed concern that with so much focus on Black male celebrities accused of crime, crime victims have been overlooked. Some focus group members mentioned the victims in the Mike Tyson, Michael Jackson, and R. Kelly cases. Veronica points out:

> With Tyson, people weren't seeing her (Desiree Washington) as somebody who needed protection. . . . When we talk about R. Kelly we don't talk about the young woman that he supposedly raped. . . . [It's] "Oh she was a young, hot girl"—even though she was fourteen and he's thirty something!

A few people expressed the opinion that there must be some way to both "protect our own" *and* acknowledge crime victims. Alicia notes that increasing the community's level of concern for victims will take some work. Based on this, she says we need to have an "informed Black protectionism. . . . There has to be a dialogue and statistics." This would include, for example, more awareness about the crime of rape—such as the types of rape (e.g., statutory, "date rape," and stranger), its prevalence, and strategies for preventing it.

Deciding how the African American community should respond to crime victims raises morality issues. Participants expressed various concerns about whether it is right to practice Black protectionism. Some participants, while not prejudging Michael Jackson's guilt or innocence in the 2005 case, wondered why he is often seen in the company of young boys. Carmen observes, "The way they (entertainers) portray themselves makes them easier to target. Like Michael, it's easy to believe that Michael does weird things behind closed doors from the way he acts in public." In reference to Marion Barry, Antwoine, a twenty-four-year-old college student, commented, "He smoked crack and got reelected. I don't know what's going on with the people in D.C. I don't want a crackhead." Michelle says that supporting someone just because they are Black sends an improper message to children:

> Parents need to start setting better examples. Children imitate what they see. So, if a parent is going to support someone just because they're Black, what kind of message does that send to their children?

Many participants agreed that Black protectionism should not be used to prop up fallen Black celebrities at the expense of Black victims and should not be used to defend conduct that is immoral.

What about the Sisters?

Overall, participants expressed support for giving protection to Black women. Interestingly, however, there was a gender division in the responses. The women expressed more concern with whether and under what circumstances Black women receive protectionism, whereas the men were more likely to defend the emphasis of Black protectionism on Black men. Alicia comments:

[The Black community is] more protective of Black males when they are attacked. When Janet Jackson was attacked I didn't see [Blacks] come to her rescue, but we went to the rescue of R. Kelly, Kobe Bryant, and O.J. Simpson. Black protectionism exists but it tends to be gender specific.

In contrast, David, a thirty-one-year-old administrator, distinguishes Janet Jackson's case from those involving Black men:

Janet Jackson didn't get the same level of support because the most severe punishment she could have received was a fine. Others were facing jail time.

Pete, who is a seventy-year-old retired professor, echoes David's sentiments that there are legitimate reasons for differentiating between Black men and Black women. He states:

One of the reasons that Black females don't get the support is that as Black men we think that they, particularly within the criminal justice system, are going to get a better shake than the Black man.

As Pete's comments highlight, concerns about how Black men are treated by the court system help explain why, as one participant noted, Black men have more "visceral" reactions to cases involving Black male celebrities who have been charged with crime.

The divergent, gender-specific views on whether Black women are entitled to Black protectionism are not dismissible as simple differences of opinion. The perspective that women need less protection than men not only affects how the African American community responds to Black women facing legal trouble, but also how it perceives Black female victims of crime. Without question, Black men are disproportionately involved in the justice system. One-third of all young Black men are in prison, on probation, or on parole. Overall, Black men, who are about 6 percent of the U.S. population, comprise almost half of those trapped by the justice system. At the same time, however, Black women are the fastest-growing group in the court system. Black women have high victimization rates for assault, murder, and rape. Although Black women are clearly tied to the justice system, as suspects and victims, because most of them are not famous, they do not appear to benefit from Black protectionism.

Support for the Common Black Person

A strong and unanticipated theme of each focus group discussion was the belief that Black protectionism should extend beyond famous Blacks—that it should protect everyday Blacks. As a group, the African American participants over age forty were quick to question why so much time and attention is focused on celebrity Blacks. Many expressed irritation and head-shaking disappointment that so many famous Blacks have gotten into legal trouble—trouble that they could have avoided. In fact, many of the over-forty participants were opposed to *talking* about Black celebrities—viewing it as a waste of time. They wanted to talk instead about how protectionism should and could be applied within local communities. Fred, fifty-two, a school district employee, asks, "Why focus on celebrities? Just because they're in the spotlight? I focus on the common person." Ebony adds, "What about the man next door?"

The view that protecting Black celebrities is futile is tied to the view that it amounts to an empty gesture. Sheila, a thirty-one-year-old graduate student, describes the downside of using Black protectionism to champion famous Blacks:

> One of the problems is that it obscures other issues that Black people should be talking about and dealing with. We concern ourselves and put so much energy into the cases of high-profile people who have plenty of money to defend themselves. However, there is a huge and growing problem with Black men and women being incarcerated in this country.

She concludes that the attention and energy that African Americans give to celebrities in trouble results in a "kind of false activism." This support may make us feel good. In the long run, however, it will have little effect on the lives of average Black folks—it will not uplift the race.

While the strength of their viewpoints varied, focus group members were in accord that there is a need to "protect our own" at home, in our local communities. For example, Brian, a forty-five-year-old business owner, said, "If you want to have protectionism, it should protect the little people." To shift the focus of Black protectionism to the common man is to shift the focus of Black protectionism away from people, to issues.

Charles comments, "The focus should be on injustice, that's what we need to concentrate on."

Many participants elaborated on the idea that remedying racial injustices should be the motivating force behind Black protectionism. For instance, several people said there is a need to apply protectionism to Blacks who are victims of police brutality. Rodney King and Amadou Diallo were used as examples of brutality victims who deserved and received wide-scale support from the African American community.

Some participants said that those who are unjustly serving prison time deserve the community's attention. Some referred specifically to people who have been wrongly convicted of crime and are serving lengthy prison terms. Others referred to the number of death row inmates who have been convicted based on faulty evidence. Others mentioned prisoners serving mandatory minimums (e.g., under the federal crack cocaine law). Related to this, a few people pointed out that there are Black political prisoners who deserve community notice and action. Assata Shakur and Mumia Abu-Jamal, whom many consider political prisoners, were two names mentioned by focus group participants. Beyond these examples, focus group members referenced the many unknown African Americans whose cases do not make the national news but who deserve the community's support—including those subject to three strike laws, those in need of effective assistance of counsel, and those entitled to a jury that represents a fair cross-section of the community.

Interracial Sex Crimes

As noted earlier, many participants expressed frustration and disgust with celebrity Blacks who get into legal trouble. There was a clear sense that high-profile Blacks need to be on guard and avoid trouble: Ebony, rhetorically, asks why those in the spotlight would "place themselves in a predicament—do something stupid and then think they can get away with it?"

Compared with the men, the women had little sympathy for Black male celebrities who had been accused of victimizing a White woman. The interracial sex crime allegations—e.g., O.J. and Kobe—evoked the most passionate responses. Referring to O.J., Alicia wryly comments, "You asked for it. You got it." Stephanie, a thirty-three-year-old office worker, shares this view, "O.J. was wrong and I'm not a racist. He crossed that line. He should have stayed where he was . . . his first wife was a Black woman." Referring to Kobe, Jasmine says, "First of all he committed adultery with a White woman. So, I have an attitude right there."

Following these comments, the women were pushed to consider whether the victim's race should matter. Some noted that the race of the victim influences their responses in individual cases. They indicated that they are less likely to be supportive or empathetic toward a famous Black male who "crosses the line." It is no secret that within the Black community there is a shortage of Black male romantic partners for Black females. Among other facts, the rising incarceration rates for Black men (higher than the rate of their college enrollment) and the increasing number of Black men who marry outside their race (much higher than the number of Black women who marry outside of their race) have made many Black women protective of Black male–Black female relationships.

Other participants pointed to the history of cases involving Black men falsely accused of sexually violating White woman—noting that these cases too often ended in lynchings, imprisonment, and families being chased out of town. The sentiment was that by crossing over to White women these men were asking for trouble. Or, at least they are partly responsible for any problems that arise.

For Blacks Only?

Should Black protectionism extend to people outside the Black community? Focus group participants were asked whether protectionism should be available to Whites, such as former president Bill Clinton. During Clinton's tenure and impeachment hearings, polls indicated that Blacks stood solidly behind him. At the peak of his ratings, the overwhelming majority of Blacks supported him.

During the discussions, many members expressed favorable views toward Clinton. One person said that he "came close to being the first Black president." Someone else commented, "He did things that benefit Black people."

There was strong support for Clinton personally, based on his stand on issues of importance to the Black community (e.g., affirmative action, AIDS funding) and his symbolic overtures (e.g., having Black friends, visiting Black churches). However, the majority commented that Black protectionism should be limited to Black people. Alicia's observation is representative of this view:

> I love Clinton and I'd vote for him again if I could, but no. No, I don't think that they (Whites) count. I feel like when we're all equal then we'll hold hands and sing, "We are the world"—but until then we are in a struggle.

Going a step further, Veronica states, "I don't think it should extend to White people because White people have something called 'White privilege.'" She elaborates by pointing out that even when Blacks are on the same level with Whites (e.g., economically and socially) they are still disadvantaged: "When a rich Black person goes out there and does something, like O.J. or Kobe, you still see race first. So it (Black wealth and fame) still doesn't equal White privilege."

However, Cynthia, a poet, who is fifty-nine, takes a more expansive view of Black protectionism. She notes that Whites have played a role in Black progress:

> There have been some White people who have protected us and I don't think there will ever be a time when we don't believe there are some good White people.

Again, most concluded that Black protectionism is "a Black thing" and should be limited to protecting Blacks in trouble. While participants suggested creating a larger net for Black protectionism, they clearly believe that protectionism should not extend to Whites. An undercurrent in the discussions was the idea that by applying protectionism exclusively to Blacks it is an acknowledgment that Blacks have special needs. This view also suggests that expanding protectionism to other racial groups will dilute its effectiveness.

Who's Black?

In discussions on eligibility for Black protectionism, participants were asked to consider, "Who's Black?" Several expressed the concern that some Blacks are getting a free pass. Specifically, it was noted that some Black stars do not identify with the African American community, yet they may still receive protectionism. Here the discussion centered on Michael Jackson, Tiger Woods, and O.J. Simpson.

In reference to Michael Jackson, participants raised questions about whether he is Black or White. Joanne, a graduate student who is twenty-three, asks, "Is Michael Jackson still Black? We were supporting him at one time. Do we consider him a lost cause?" Malik comments, "Michael Jackson is a race issue unto himself." Although questions were raised about the changes in Jackson's physical appearance and his racial consciousness, it was obvious from the discussions that participants consider him Black. Overall, however, in discussing protectionism, Michael Jackson's case served more as a source of comic relief than a case for serious analysis.

Antwoine commented that although Tiger Woods "says he's not Black," the Black community would "probably be around to provide him support" if he was accused of a crime. Alicia expressed concern that some Blacks, such as O.J., are Black when it is "convenient." While participants observed that some Blacks may not consider themselves Black and are distant from the community, there was no clear consensus as to how they should be treated, regarding the availability of protectionism.

Political Matters

Participants were asked to consider how the African American community benefits from supporting people like O.J., Clarence Thomas, or R. Kelly. Specifically, they were asked whether there should be a political litmus test in applying protectionism. Should community members consider a person's politics, such as whether they are progressive, moderate, or conservative on social issues, when deciding whether to grant protectionism? Should it matter whether the person considers themselves part of the community (e.g., where they live), whether they make donations to charitable causes, or the substance of their public statements? Without some strings attached, Black protectionism is arguably a kind of voyeuristic support. As Malik notes, protectionism currently works as a way "to come together without really sticking out our necks." It costs nothing and because it is so freely given, its overall impact is diminished.

In response to the question of the role that politics should play, most agreed that politics should be a factor. Christina comments:

> Ideally it should be based on what we already know about that individual and how they contribute to the Black community, what they're doing for us as a people.

Sheila agrees, "I do apply a political litmus test and I wish more people would be more critical about who to support. . . . Black celebrities who do not identify with our community should be treated differently." Antwoine compares cases to make his point:

> Jesse Jackson is giving back to people who are still struggling. O.J. or Tiger, they haven't done anything. What has Kobe done for the community? Why should I . . . support him when he hasn't done anything except make baskets? His shoes cost $100, a portion of that goes to him, none of that to the community.

Similar comments were made about Clarence Thomas—that he has done little to earn the community's embrace. Another person voiced support for considering the public policy implications of supporting someone.

At least one participant, however, felt that a grant of Black protectionism should not be limited to those who "give back" in traditional ways to the Black community (e.g., financial contributions, local appearances). Accordingly, being successful, famous, and Black should be enough by itself to trigger Black protectionism. Michelle says that high-profile Blacks "give hope"—they show the community what is possible. This is particularly true for those celebrities who had to fight to overcome obstacles to achieve success (e.g., poverty, abuse, mainstream rejection) to become successful. Because hope is a valuable and much needed community resource, it is sufficient to justify supporting a fallen celebrity.

Overall, however, there was agreement that community members should factor in one's actions, political and general, in deciding whether to apply Black protectionism. Also, at least with regard to celebrities, most said that the community should hold their feet to the fire.

The Permanence of Black Protectionism

In response to the question of whether there would ever be a time when we would not have Black protectionism, most participants concluded that it would be here for a long time. Comments fell into two camps: either Black protectionism will always exist, or Black protectionism will eventually disappear.

Some, including Simone, twenty-four, believe that the persistence of racism means the persistence of Black protectionism: "It will probably be around for a very, very, very long time because racism is probably going to stick around for a very, very, very long time." Christina offers, "Black protectionism is going to exist as long as we can tell who's Black and who's not." Jermaine noted that an increase in the number of Blacks might signal a decline in protectionism; specifically, that protectionism will erode when Blacks are in the majority—when that happens Blacks will be less likely to believe that our Black leaders and entertainers are being targeted by the system. Alicia, however, disagreed with this perspective, "This country was founded on racism . . . the language, the laws, the education, the financial system are all based on oppression. So, even if the population changes [the history doesn't change]."

Analysis

Five clear themes emerged from the focus group discussions. First, the majority of participants agreed that Black protectionism exists. Second, most agreed that it represents an important response to historical and contemporary forms of oppression against African Americans, particularly within the U.S. criminal court system. Third, most believe that protectionism should be applied selectively. They would expand it to protect "the little guy"—people in the local communities whose cases do not make national headlines. As well, many supported the idea of including more Black women within the protected class. Additionally, a few participants said they want protectionism to embrace Black crime victims—concluding that an all-out embrace of Black protectionism has the effect of treating the victim as suspect, rather than the system. There was also concern that unrestricted Black protectionism sends the message that African Americans are more concerned with protecting celebrities than addressing crime within the community. Fourth, there was a strong, clear sentiment that protectionism should only be available for Blacks. While noting that many Whites are involved in the fight for racial justice, most felt that protectionism should be the sole province of African Americans. Fifth, most agreed that applying Black protectionism should include a political calculus. This would mean some consideration of whether the potential recipient's past actions indicate an interest and concern for the African American community at large.

In addition to the above themes, there were some gaps and inconsistencies in the discussions of Black protectionism. First, many said that it would be a good idea to use protectionism to embrace Black victims and Black women in particular. At the same time, however, several people expressed a strong allegiance to fallen male celebrities. The belief that there is a conspiracy to bring down Black men or, minimally, a "force" that makes it hard for Black men to succeed, made many participants sympathetic and ultimately protective of Black men—even those who engaged in crime. Related to this, many were surprised to learn that as a group Black women do not benefit from Black protectionism. Many simply were not aware that Black protectionism is almost entirely skewed to protect Black men and thus had not considered the gender-based implications of this reality.

Second, in discussing the cases, it was clear that at least some participants were working with incorrect facts. This came out most starkly in discussions about the Mike Tyson case. One focus group member adamantly insisted that a woman who goes to a hotel room late at night to visit a man has consented to have sex. Another insisted that Anita Hill, Clarence Thomas's accuser, was "set up" by White feminists. Also, as noted earlier, to apply Black protectionism discriminately, more community members need to gather more factual information in specific cases. For some African Americans this may require more attention to case-specific details and perhaps expanding their sources of information.

Conclusion

The detailed and wide-ranging focus group discussions add texture to the overall analysis of Black protectionism. It is clear that those community members who were interviewed are concerned about issues of racial justice. They also believe that if it was available to a larger pool of Blacks and applied more rigorously, Black protectionism could be an effective tool, another step toward fighting for racial equality.

Comments by Malik and Kenny provide representative closing remarks. On the existence of protectionism, Malik states, "It's natural for a group, that has its own identity and is attacked on the basis of that same identity, to form a sense of protectionism." On the value of protectionism Kenny concludes:

> It gives us a voice to the dominant society. It tells White people here we are and that we're not going to let them, no matter what, establish laws

and prejudices without us uniting and saying we are a body and we're going to bind together.

The focus group discussions add context and depth to the polls and surveys on the Black community's opinion in cases involving Black celebrities charged with crime. The conversations offer clear directions on how Black protectionism can be reworked and redefined to reflect the broad concerns, interests, and goals of the African American community.

WE WANT BLACK POWER

AP/Wide World

THE GOOD, THE BAD, AND THE UGLY

Introduction

In an earlier chapter the nuts and bolts of Black protectionism are explored. Specifically, who gets it, which mechanisms trigger it, when is it available, and how it works. As well, the chapter on focus groups examines how some members of the African American community view the practice of protectionism. What remains to be answered is "So what?" What does it mean to say that Blacks as a group overwhelmingly support famous Blacks who are charged with criminal activity? More to the point, what is the *value* of Black protectionism? What are its costs and what are its benefits? A critique of its application, the focus of this chapter, will provide some insights on its fault lines. This analysis makes it possible to reconfigure Black protectionism so that it can operate as a force for racial justice.

Benefits of Black Protectionism

Black protectionism has four interrelated benefits. First, it reinforces group solidarity. When applied, it provides a common ground upon which Blacks can stand. Black protectionism allows for a demonstration of group strength and unity at a time when the group is still viewed as politically, economically, and socially marginal. Related to this, protectionism acts as a racial buffer for Blacks. It sends a message within the community that African Americans are not the stereotypes they are portrayed to be in the mainstream media. At the same time, Black protectionism allows the community to say to larger society, "You may see us as outcasts, but we, members of the community, know differently."

Second, Black protectionism allows African Americans to weigh and balance numerous factors before determining whether to provide support to a prominent African American. The Black community can compare the cost of an individual's moral or criminal lapse (e.g., assault, adultery, pedophilia, or drug use) against the benefit of an individual's "good acts." This permits African Americans to make a distinction between what a person does in his public life and what a person does in his private life (e.g., Marion Barry, Jesse Jackson, and R. Kelly). Beyond looking at the actions of the potential recipient of Black protectionism, the community is also affected by other factors. Considerations include the history of race relations and how Blacks fare in society today, compared with Whites. It could be argued that Black protectionism reflects a sophisticated analysis of race, crime, and justice in America. Perhaps the existing approach, which favors granting Black protectionism, is the result of the relatively small number of Black politicians and celebrities. Black protectionism offers a way to resurrect African Americans who get into legal trouble. By doing so, it allows the Black elite to maintain its exalted status within the community.

Third, Black protectionism acts as a sociopolitical statement. It states that while conditions may have improved for Blacks, they have not improved that much. Racial protectionism serves as a reminder that historical forms of racial discrimination—e.g., slavery, slave codes, Black laws, lynching, Black codes, and Jim Crow—have contemporary manifestations, such as racial profiling, hate crimes, and police brutality. Thus, Black protectionism offers a contrasting view to mainstream assessments of racial progress. At a time when the Black community is routinely and rhetorically asked whether race relations are better today than they were fifty years ago, Black protectionism boldly responds by saying that race relations still have a long way to go. In this way, it serves as a history lesson. Each case of Black protectionism opens the door for America to discuss its lengthy history of anti-Black racism. Opportunities for a broad, public discussion of this history are few and far between.

Fourth, the existence of Black protectionism raises questions about the law's legitimacy. The fact that Blacks as a group are quick to minimize criminal charges against some members of the community indicates that concerns about racial bias persist. In essence, the practice of Black protectionism challenges the validity and signals the ineffectiveness of a legal system that profiles and punishes on the basis of race. Thus, Black protectionism operates as a form of agency. It allows Blacks themselves to decide whether someone within the community should be subject to public ridicule, sanction, and labeled an outcast. The existence of protectionism is a clear rejection of the status quo. It represents the Black community's voice stating unequivocally that African Americans themselves will decide who is entitled to community protection and who is not. Protectionism operates as a racial filter through which African Americans can view other Blacks who have achieved mainstream success.

Black protectionism acts as both an internal force within the Black community, fostering group solidarity, and as an external force, sending a message to outsiders. It acts as a race-relations barometer, an index of where the Black community and the White community are on issues of race and racism. The need for Black protectionism reinforces itself each time a prominent Black is accused of wrongdoing and the White mainstream is perceived as being overzealous in its reaction (e.g., the O.J. Simpson case) or as applying a guilty-until-proven-innocent analysis (e.g., the Marion Barry and Michael Jackson cases). Each case acts to widen and deepen the already existing racial chasm.

Costs of Black Protectionism

While Black protectionism has some obvious benefits, there are also many problematic features. One troubling feature is that protectionism does not acknowledge or punish wrongdoing and does not factor in the potential recipient's political allegiance to the Black community. Another problematic aspect is that it promotes the idea that the Black community has an identifiable and static viewpoint. As such, Black protectionism promotes the practice of blind racial loyalty. Just as questionable, protectionism is sometimes triggered by Black celebrities themselves. It also offers one type of support to Black men and another, lesser type, to Black women. Ultimately, these myriad costs impact the effectiveness of protectionism and jeopardize its chances of creating positive community change.

No Sanction, No Accountability

One of the most striking things about Black protectionism is that it appears to be unaffected by culpability. Even in those instances where it is undisputed that the person engaged in wrongdoing, Black protectionism may still work. The Jesse Jackson and Marion Barry incidents are cases in point. When news surfaced that Jackson had fathered a child with his mistress, he issued a straightforward acknowledgment of paternity.[1] In Barry's case, his drug use was captured on videotape and authenticated by his reaction after law enforcement stormed his hotel room: "[The] bitch set me up."[2]

Arguably, one of the costs of Black protectionism is its failure to differentiate between those who have engaged in misconduct and those who have not. This is a cost given that Black protectionism developed primarily as a response to the false criminal charges that were routinely leveled against Black men. Overlooking culpability is particularly worrisome when there is no sanction for wrongdoing.

Further, a grant of protectionism does not impose any quid pro quo. For instance, a person who receives Black protectionism does not have to apologize for his transgression, donate money to a worthy cause, or in any other way support the African American community. Simply put, recipients, whether innocent or guilty, are not required to *do* anything. Black protectionism is a gift with no strings attached.

Before looking at the reasons for the lack of accountability, it is worth considering whether fallen Black celebrities *should* be required to do something. The argument that Black protectionism should impose some type of sanction is an acknowledgment of what should be a dynamic relationship between the African American community and the person facing mainstream scrutiny.

One view is that well-known Blacks who have engaged in wrongdoing have let the community down. If celebrities are representative of the community, each time there is a celebrity allegation of crime, the community is held to answer. This makes the famous person (guilty or innocent) indebted to community members who shoulder this burden. Community members are likely to defend the person while the mainstream media uses the incident as further proof of the link between Blacks and crime. The fallen celebrity, then, should repay this debt to the African American community. Repayment of this debt should not be demanded but strongly encouraged. It is likely that once the community tailors its use of Black protectionism to shield only those who have served the community, accountability will be easier to achieve.

There are several possible explanations for the absence of sanctions.[3] First, for some African Americans, the harsh actions of government officials, such as police officers or prosecutors, mitigate or completely excuse the accused person's offense. In the Marion Barry case, for instance, many African Americans considered the fact that the government targeted Barry. This fact was weighed against his videotaped drug use. Because many people concluded that on balance, the government's actions were more culpable than Barry's, Black protectionism was able to take a firm hold.

Second, there is a strong belief that what a person does in his private life should not be used to undermine his professional capabilities. This viewpoint was evident during the Bill Clinton, Jesse Jackson, and Barry scandals. With Clinton and Barry, some people categorized their cases as "family matters" and concluded that any problems should be resolved between the husband and wife. If their wives forgive their husbands' transgressions then there is no need for a public sanction. The public versus private distinction has also been a clear thread of public discourse in the R. Kelly case. This is evident in comments such as "I don't know what R. Kelly does in his private life. I just know he makes great music." All told, African Americans appear unwilling to come down hard on famous Blacks for an incident, particularly one based on circumstantial evidence, that can be dismissed as a private or personal matter.

Third, many African Americans believe that whenever a well-known Black person is charged with a crime they will be subjected to a public shaming process. That is, the charges are broadcast across various news outlets, questions are raised about the person's accomplishments, talking heads denounce the person, and the person is ridiculed on late-night talk shows. For many African Americans, this public hazing ritual is punishment enough and there is no need for the community to "pile on." Also, many Blacks believe that any judgment, reprimand, or sanction is best left to a higher power.

Fourth, as noted earlier, the degree to which Black protectionism is applied in a particular case depends on a range of factors. As the trigger questions indicate (see chapter 3), Blacks weigh various factors, including the degree of the government's overreaching, the degree of the alleged harm, and whether the accused has performed "good acts." For instance, for a person who has a stockpile of Black support based on his political affiliations, community service, or position, the Black community is much more likely to lay out the Black protectionism welcome mat. So, the failure to impose any accountability may be partially based on the fact that the person has already paid their race dues. The cases involving Marion Barry, Bill Clinton, and Jesse Jackson are useful examples. The question remains, how does the Black community benefit from providing no-strings-attached Black protectionism in these three cases? Would the application of Black protectionism yield greater long-term benefits if more were required of its beneficiaries?

Fifth, although it is rarely stated openly, it appears that many people believe that those individuals who reach a certain level of material wealth or fame—whether they are Black or White—should not be held to the same standards as everyone else. More to the point, this view suggests that the rich and famous should be treated as less culpable than the nonrich and nonfamous. Black protectionism exemplifies this double standard. It asserts that if famous Whites can get off the hook for serious crimes, then so should famous Blacks. Right or wrong, high-achieving Blacks are entitled to the same privileges as high-achieving Whites. Expressions of this sentiment were stated openly following the Simpson acquittal.

All told, the Black community's all-forgiving attitude stands in stark contrast to past community practices. Protectionism was used to protect against false charges of crime (e.g., murder and rape) that were made against someone Black. Legions of false rape allegations that resulted in lynching have been documented. Again, Black protectionism originated to protect community members against criminal lies told about Black men. Under these circumstances, there was no need to impose a sanction because there had been no wrongdoing. In many of the contemporary cases of Black protectionism, however, the prominent Black person is guilty of the crime he was charged with (e.g., Marion Barry, Melvin Reynolds, Bill Clinton, and Jesse Jackson).

Interestingly, the historical record shows that Blacks engaged in forms of vigilante justice to protect the Black community and deter future harm against its members. During Reconstruction, the Black community punished Blacks who committed crimes. E. M. Beck and Stewart Tolnay document cases involving intraracial lynching—*Blacks who lynched other Blacks.* They analyze 129 cases of Black-on-Black lynchings between 1882 and

1930. In these cases, Blacks sought retribution against other Blacks who committed crimes against the community, such as murder, rape, and assault. Although the lynch victims were not "famous," the intraracial sanctions analyzed by Beck and Tolnay reflect a time when the African American community recognized the value of race-based community sanctions.[4]

Black protectionism's failure to delineate between the presence of wrongdoing and the absence of wrongdoing creates yet another problem. It means that protectionism may work to favor someone who has engaged in crime (e.g., Marion Barry), while at the same time denying it to someone who clearly has not (e.g., Lani Guinier and Joycelyn Elders). This inconsistency exists because Black protectionism has neither guidelines nor rules. This means that Black protectionism, ostensibly used to thwart unfair racial attacks, can result in a rough justice.

The fact that Black protectionism embraces the innocent and guilty alike substantially undercuts its legitimacy. It works to protect a select group of African Americans but does not impose upon them any community responsibilities or dues. It does not, at a minimum, require an apology to the community from those who are guilty of wrongdoing. As a consequence, Black protectionism is missing a crucial component, accountability.

Apolitical and Colorless

African Americans across the political spectrum have benefited from protectionism. The politically neutral application of protectionism raises an important question: Is it beneficial to the Black community to rally behind someone who does not adopt a mainstream civil rights agenda? How, for example, did the Black community benefit from supporting someone such as Clarence Thomas, who is opposed to affirmative action? It could be argued that the collective embrace of Thomas did more harm than good. In his first decade on the U.S. Supreme Court, Thomas consistently voted against laws that protected hard-won civil rights and liberties.[5]

Cornel West observes that Thomas's assertion of racial authenticity, combined with the "closing ranks mentality" of Blacks and the appeal of Black nationalism, resulted in the political hoodwinking of Black America.[6] This practice, West argues, results in race superseding gender: "The idea of black people closing ranks against hostile white Americans reinforces black male power exercised over black women."[7] As currently applied, Black protectionism precludes a nuanced assessment of race and gender relations. By applying a more thoughtful critique, West concludes that "both Thomas and Hill would be viewed as two black Republican conservative supporters of some of the most vicious policies to besiege black working and poor communities since Jim and Jane Crow segregation."[8]

A similar conclusion could be reached about the O.J. Simpson case. The communal embrace of Simpson yielded little tangible benefit to African Americans as a group. Chris Rock captures this reality in his insightful take on the not-guilty verdict in the Simpson case:

> Black people too happy, White people too mad. White people were like, "Man this is bullshit." I ain't seen White people that mad since they canceled M*A*S*H. Black people are like "Yeah, we won!" What the fuck did we win? Everyday I look in my mailbox for my O.J. prize—nothin'![9]

As already noted, Black protectionism is not given in exchange for a community gain or a prize. Rather, it may reflect stakes of another kind. According to Michael Eric Dyson, the Black community's strong support for Simpson may indicate the group's refusal to play the "race authenticity game."[10] In this game, Dyson explains, only "'real' Blacks deserve support when racial difficulties arise."[11] Dyson concludes that the Black embrace of O.J. "can be read less charitably . . . as the automatic embrace of a fallen figure simply because he is Black."[12] Overall, both the Thomas and Simpson cases demonstrate that knee-jerk protectionism may have few long-term benefits.

In addition to its failure to weigh political affiliation, Black protectionism also ignores one's degree of racial pride or identification with Blackness. Michael Jackson's case underscores this point. Through radical cosmetic surgery, Jackson—who was very attractive as a young man—has eliminated all traces of his former trademark African American racial features, including brown skin color, full lips, and a broad nose. In addition to this, Jackson promotes colorlessness in his music. For instance, his song, "Black or White," includes the lyrics: "See it's not about races, just places" and "I'm not going to spend my life being a color."[13] Jackson is also the father of three White-looking children, who do not appear to have any African American racial features. Years before he was charged with murder, Simpson, too, expressed his desire to be viewed in nonracial terms[14] (see chapter 1).

Related to the question of how politics impacts a grant of Black protectionism, Kobe Bryant's case presents an interesting issue. As discussed earlier, at the Teen Choice Awards Bryant wore a Muhammad Ali T-shirt and upon accepting his award, he paraphrased a Martin Luther King Jr. quote[15] (see chapter 3). Bryant's dress and comment are notable because he steered clear of political or racial statements before his arrest. Bryant's invocation of not one but two revered Black civil rights heroes was a transparent call for Black support. These references were an over-the-top attempt to borrow King and Ali's political credibility. Further, by implying that he had been unfairly charged, Bryant sought to garner Black sympathy and support.

Oddly, the fact that a potential recipient of Black protectionism may not identify with the Black community, may not see himself as Black, or might not promote the uplift of African Americans, does not preclude protectionism. It is odd because Black protectionism, by definition, is all about race. It would seem that at a minimum, in order to receive protection, one would have to readily identify oneself as African American or promote causes directly tied to advancing the Black community. Arguably, to do otherwise is to allow those outside the community to determine who is Black and who represents the community. As the above discussion makes clear, however, Blacks, whether they are Black-identified, colorless, conservative, progressive, or apolitical, are shielded by Black protectionism's oversized umbrella.

The Black Monolith

Another potential cost of Black protectionism is that it portrays the African American community as a monolith—one body, one voice. This raises two overlapping concerns. First, it presents a false reality. In truth, there are diverse viewpoints within the African American community. The sweep of Black protectionism casts aside alternate viewpoints. In part, this occurs because the media interprets the support of the Black majority as representative of the entire group.

The same myth was at play in the Mike Tyson case. Tyson had the support of most Blacks, who thought he was unfairly charged and convicted of rape. As noted previously, when Tyson returned from prison his supporters planned a welcome home rally. While the media focused on Black support for Tyson's release, it largely overlooked dissenters. For example, there were many Blacks who took a stand against Tyson in particular and sexual abuse against Black women in general. Newspaper ads were placed and counterrallies were held to protest sexual assault against Black women.

Second, within the Black community, protectionism not only masks alternative viewpoints, it discourages them. It drowns out the voices of dissenters, who are perceived as airing dirty laundry. As currently practiced, then, Black protectionism encourages noncritical perspectives. Specifically, it fosters reflex responses to criminal charges against a famous Black person. Today's version of Black protectionism practically forces all Blacks to fall in line with the majority of Blacks.

The myth that all Blacks think and perceive the world in one way is enhanced each time Black protectionism is invoked. This myth erases the subtlety and nuance of applying Black protectionism—one of its initial selling points (see the discussion of the trigger questions in chapters 1 and 4). In its current form, Black protectionism promotes the false notion that the Black community speaks with one voice. This places the entire community in a tight-fitting box, one that cannot hold those who think outside of it.

Blind Loyalty

The African American community's response to Bill Clinton offers an exemplar for assessing whether Black protectionism at times works against Black interests. Making sense of the community's steadfast support for Clinton requires a history lesson. DeWayne Wickham observes:

> [T]o fully understand Clinton's appeal to blacks you must first juxtapose him to the forty-one men—from George Washington to George Bush—who preceded him in the presidency. It is impossible to explain Clinton's popularity with African Americans without first probing the relationship that blacks have had with this nation's long line of chief executives.[16]

There are many reasons that the Black community rallied behind President Clinton—offering increased support as he weathered impeachment. As noted, Clinton appeared empathetic to Black struggles against racism, had himself triumphed over difficult beginnings, appointed record numbers of African Americans to executive and judicial posts, and appeared genuinely comfortable in the company of Blacks. Ron Walters argues that the embrace of Clinton further tightened as the country witnessed an upsurge in White nationalism. According to Walters, this increased Black political identity with Clinton and the sense that Blacks and Clinton were in the same foxhole.[17]

On the other hand, a detailed critique of Clinton's record on race and the justice system reveals some noteworthy findings. Most notably, it was during his presidency that the nation's most punitive crime bill was signed into law.[18] In *The Debt*, Randall Robinson criticizes the Black community's open embrace of Clinton. Robinson notes that the Black community welcomes leaders who appear outwardly friendly toward Blacks, even when they do not have their best interests at heart.[19] After a discussion of some of Clinton's policies, including a harsh welfare reform bill, Robinson concludes that Blacks are satisfied with symbolic gestures. Consequently, Clinton was able to tap into the Black well of support by having high visibility in Black churches, having Black friends, taking trips to Africa, and appointing a race relations panel.

As the above discussion reflects, there are strong factors that argue for and against a grant of Black protectionism to Clinton. What matters most in a decision to extend Black protectionism is that at a minimum there should be *some* analysis. It should not reflect a victory of "personality over policy."[20] A responsible, critical application of Black protectionism takes work. Black support for Clinton looked to be reflexive rather than analytical. A critical assessment of the appropriateness of Black protectionism in a particular case may divide the community. After all, reasonable minds may disagree. However, this is a far better outcome than a "united" community that has not taken the time to evaluate the costs and benefits of granting group protection.

Blind loyalty applies most often to cases where the person has expressed a strong allegiance to the Black community. In an analysis of African American support for Bill Clinton and Marion Barry, Ta-Nehisi Coates notes that Black men with a "deep resume of political activism" will find support within the Black community.[21] Notably, blind loyalty is triggered in those cases where the prominent Black person has paid their "race dues" (e.g., politicians who promote a Black civil rights agenda or Blacks who embrace their Blackness). In this way, blind loyalty cases differ from those where protectionism is used to protect Blacks who are apolitical (e.g., politics undefined) or "colorless."

Coates observes that both Clinton and Barry showed affection for African Americans, a group that is largely ignored by Washington's power elite. The two men are labeled "soul mates," based on their indiscretions and the Black community's response to them. Coates argues that both politicians received a "moral pass from [Blacks] who specialize in offering redemption to wayward souls." With little effort, Clinton and Barry were able to capitalize on the Black community's palpable need for attention and recognition.

Black protectionism persists as a way for Blacks to say they are worthy of compassion, trust, and constitutional protection. Leonard Pitts, in an editorial discussing African American support for R. Kelly, summarizes the harm of blind race loyalty:

> [W]e are often indiscriminate . . . expending energy and political capital regardless of who is in trouble or why. Regardless of anything, except that he or she is Black. . . . It makes us seem . . . predictable. And reflexive. . . . We—African Americans—ought to be more thoughtful about who we choose to rally around, ought to be less automatic in leaping to the defense.[22]

Noncritical race loyalty does little to advance racial justice. It does not embolden the Black community. It rewards the person in trouble for being Black. In many cases, this person betrayed the community in the first place (by committing an indiscretion or offense). As discussed earlier, without any sanctions, blind race loyalty yields little community benefit because it does not deter future bad acts by the person in trouble.

The Celebrity Trigger

In some instances Black celebrities themselves play a key role in initiating Black protectionism. As well, sometimes celebrities themselves (or their representatives) invoke protectionism (e.g., Kobe Bryant and Michael Jackson). When celebrities go to the defense of other famous African Americans, this sends a direct message to the rest of the community that an injustice has occurred. This might also be an offensive move—that Black celebrities speak out in the hopes that someone would speak on their behalf, if necessary. This should come as no surprise. After all, who would *not* want a Black safety net? In my discussion of Black protectionism with Tavis Smiley (on his former National Public Radio show) he said that he hoped that he would never do anything to warrant Black protectionism. However, if he is ever in need, Smiley wryly added, "I want some."[23]

Several concerns are raised when celebrities invoke Black protectionism. First, there are no clear rules for when Black protectionism will be applied. In the case of one celebrity speaking on behalf of another, are they for instance, returning a favor or defending an innocent friend? In other words, is the call for protectionism legitimate? Second, prominent Blacks run the political gamut (as is true for the not-so-famous). As a result, it cannot be assumed that the person calling for Black protectionism is interested in racial uplift or community advancement. The fact that Black celebrities are sometimes the trigger for protectionism may partly explain why Black protectionism has been depoliticized—in stark contrast to its early roots. Of course, it may be that celebrities are filling in for absent Black political leaders. Whatever the reason, Black protectionism should be triggered by the community, acting in its own best interest, not by individuals—who may not have an identifiable, embraceable Black political agenda.

For Men Only?

What can we make of Black protectionism's near exclusion of Black women? It is remarkable that so few Black women have been able to tap into the deep well of Black support. One obvious reason is the fact that very few famous Black women have faced serious criminal charges (e.g., murder or sexual assault)—certainly none as well-known and loved as either O.J. Simpson, Mike Tyson, or Michael Jackson. This makes comparisons across gender difficult.

Another reason for the Black community's lack of interest in cases involving Black women, compared with cases involving Black men, may be the role of "race dues." For instance, a review of the cases involving politicians and political appointees indicates that these Black women had little name recognition, compared with the Black men who received protectionism. While Jesse Jackson, Marion Barry, Melvin Reynolds, and Bill Clinton are nationally recognized as advocates for Black civil rights, Carol Moseley-Braun, Joycelyn Elders, Lani Guinier, and Alexis Herman were not as well-known for their civil rights work (at the time of the allegations). This perception existed despite the reality that each of these women had worked for years to improve conditions within the Black community. Guinier, for instance, has had a long history of legal activism in the struggle for civil rights. However, at the time of the nomination, her work was not well-known outside of legal circles.

To test the "race dues" hypothesis there would need to be a case involving a Black woman whose civil rights track record was known and respected, someone such as congresswoman and civil rights veteran Maxine Waters. The Black community's response to a felony charge against Waters would provide an ideal test of the role of gender in the operation of Black protectionism. If Black protectionism did not extend to someone such as Waters, it would be undeniable that something more than race dues is at work.

As noted, it might also be that whoever qualifies first for Black protectionism "wins." So, because Thomas was the first to stake a claim to the Black community's loyalty he received protectionism. As noted earlier, the gender variable cannot be overlooked. It is not certain that if Anita Hill had been "first" that she would have received support over Thomas. A third possibility is that in matters of Black protectionism, gender trumps race. Where the competition for Black protectionism involves a Black man who is "up against" a Black woman, the Black man will always "win." The Clarence Thomas hearings highlight the complex interactions between race, gender, and loyalty. The pro-Thomas response makes a compelling argument that issues of gender take a back seat to issues of race. For example, where a prominent Black man faces allegations of wrongdoing, within-race gender issues are dismissed as trifling, inside skirmishes and are marginalized to protect the larger societal threat to Black men. A complete test of the effect of gender on Black protectionism has yet to come. It remains to be seen how the Black community would respond to a case involving a Black man who accuses a famous Black woman of criminal conduct, or as noted, one involving a famous Black woman who accuses a Black man of criminal conduct.

Pinpointing gender bias as the culprit, however, answers one question. Another question is *why* are Black men "privileged" over Black women? At a book reading where I discussed Black protectionism, an audience member commented that perhaps Black protectionism favors Black men because many people believe that Black men *need* it more than Black women. Whichever statistical measure is used—economic, education, incarceration, employment, political, or health—Black men are under siege. By contrast, Black women, the argument goes, are not under siege. As "two-fers," Black women are less threatening and are preferred over Black men in the workplace. Therefore, the argument continues, when prominent Black men face legal trouble, unlike Black women, they need the community's boundless support.

There are of course competing views of how Black women actually fare in U.S. society. For example, discussions of violence within the Black community typically focus on Black men. In their book, *Gender Talk*, Johnnetta Betsch Cole and Beverly Guy-Sheftall observe that there is relatively little focus on violence against Black women: "[T]his perpetuates the idea that Black male bodies are more at risk than those of Black women and children."[24] They go on to observe that historically Black men were not the only lynch victims. "We do not have [in the public discourse] although we know she existed, a Black female counterpart, for example, to the graphic visual images conjured up by our memories of the lynching death of . . . Emmett Till."[25]

Competing views of Black women are typically accompanied by additional statistics. For instance, a look at rising incarceration rates for Black women, bottom-tier wages, numbers on public assistance, rising and disproportionate rates of female heads-of-households, domestic violence, out of wedlock births, HIV/AIDS infection, obesity, and high school dropout rates, show that Black women, too, could use the same helping hand that has been extended to Black men.

The above analysis demonstrates that as currently practiced, Black protectionism works at cross purposes. On the one hand it serves as a race guard for many prominent Black men who face legal trouble. On the other hand it singles out Black men as a special class, a class more worthy and deserving of privileged treatment than others. It almost completely shuts the door on Black women. Inherent in this Black male essentialist perspective, however, is a problem of focus. In the long term, Black protectionism will work most effectively if it is designed to promote racial justice and is not simply a visceral reaction to the latest Black male celebrity charged with a crime.

Some Victims Are Better Than Others

Another issue related to the dynamic process of Black protectionism—a process that works to protect Black men—is the issue of how Black protectionism defines "victim." Black protectionism sends a message that some victims deserve more support than others. First, it expands the definition of victim. For instance, a famous Black man who is charged with a crime may be classified as a "victim of the system." In essence, it privileges some victims over others.

Second, Black protectionism primarily works to cloak famous Blacks. In this way the message is sent that the Black community will stand up and support prominent Black men charged with crime at a much higher level than they would the average Black man who has been victimized by crime (e.g., someone who was robbed or assaulted). In effect, it protects well-to-do Blacks. Thus, Black protectionism has a class bias. This is a major weakness. According to a July 2003 report by the Justice Department, young African American men are more likely to be crime victims than members of any other race and gender group. They are also more likely to face a violent death than members of other race and gender groups.

Third, Black protectionism imposes a victim hierarchy. Again, it is instructive to examine how protectionism treats Black men compared with Black women. The Clarence Thomas hearings offer a classic case. Within the Black community, Thomas was widely viewed as a victim of a false charge of sexual harassment—charges that in the past led Whites to lynch thousands of Black men (who were falsely accused of assaulting White women). Cole and Guy-Sheftall assess how Black women and Black men are sized up against each other in a zero-sum game of race and gender politics. In their analysis of the Thomas hearings, they observe that this history weighed heavily on how Thomas and Hill were perceived. Thomas was viewed as the victim of a corrupt justice system that unfairly paints Black men as sexual predators. If Hill was seen as a victim at all, she was seen as a victim of a relatively minor crime. On balance, the crimes against Thomas were considered more serious and more threatening to the African American community than those against Hill. Cole and Guy-Sheftall state:

> Hill should have been able to "represent" the race as well [as Thomas] because of the historical sexual abuse of Black women, but we do not attach the same significance to the racial experiences of Black women. The lynching of Black males remains the quintessential marker of racial subordination and the undeniable evidence of the "truth" that Black men are the primary victims of white supremacy.[26]

They conclude that as a Black man, Thomas held the "political ace" and Hill "could not mobilize the Black community . . . for the 'lesser' crime of sexual harassment."[27] Thus, Thomas, not Hill, was allowed to embody

"Blackness" because on balance the community's fear of Black men being lynched by a White mob was more important than its concern with the sexual harassment of a Black woman by a Black man.

Currently Black protectionism splits the Black community by gender. It treats prominent Black men as a unique class and leaves well-known Black women to fend for themselves. Other considerations besides gender should weigh more heavily in a determination of whether to grant Black protectionism. The bottom line calculation has to be based on what is in the community's best interests. Or, more specifically, a determination of whether "rallying around the brother" promotes racial justice. To be viable, a grant of Black protectionism must be specific not general. And, so long as Black protectionism is given to O.J. Simpson, but not Lani Guinier or Joycelyn Elders, it misses its opportunity to further the goals of racial equality.

External Consequences

Ever-Present Black Protectionism

One result of the unwieldy application of Black protectionism is that it may *appear* to operate even when it does not. An interview with comedian Rosie O'Donnell reveals an interesting instance of this problem. In her May 2004 appearance on Barbara Walter's ABC show, *The View*, O'Donnell, who is White, lamented the fact that more women did not come to the defense of home-style entrepreneur Martha Stewart: "What the federal government said is that you can take the number one woman in America, take her down for thirty grand and the women won't stand up and scream." O'Donnell then went on to state, "[H]ere's what I love. The Black community said you cannot have O.J. Simpson, you cannot have Jayson Williams" (see appendix). O'Donnell's comments provoked a heated response from the show's African American cohost, Star Jones. Jones noted that there were only two Blacks on the jury that declined to convict Williams of the manslaughter charges. Jones asked rhetorically, "When did Black people have a meeting and vote?"[28]

O'Donnell's linking of Simpson and Williams is intriguing. While Simpson clearly received Black protectionism, the same is not true for Williams. The Williams case received a lot of media attention. However, there is no indication that Blacks rallied behind him. Public commentary by African Americans typically ranged from disbelief to anger at Williams's poor judgment (e.g., his failure to immediately call the police after accidentally shooting his chauffeur). Thus, O'Donnell's remarks reflect her *assumption* that Williams received Black protectionism—perhaps because he was not convicted of the most serious offense. Although inaccurate, her assumption is not surprising given the widespread grant of protectionism to so many famous Blacks.

"Playing the Race Card" and the Politics of Race

How does the practice of Black protectionism affect how Blacks as a group are viewed by mainstream society? Up to this point, I have not addressed this issue in my analysis of Black protectionism. This is because the major thrust of this discussion is properly focused on how to make Black protectionism work for the community it is designed to protect. Part of an overall assessment, however, requires at least some discussion of how people outside the group view Black protectionism.

One major thread running through the responses to Black protectionism is that Blacks are playing the race card whenever they say that race may have been a factor in the arrest, charge, or prosecution of a famous Black person. Seeds of the "race card" are evident in White responses to the Kobe Bryant, Sean Combs, Mike Tyson, Michael Jackson, and Clarence Thomas cases.

The choice of the language, "playing the race card," to describe someone (typically a Black person) who raises the issue of race in a criminal or civil case is telling. Obviously the expression is used to deflect attention from the issue of race itself. But it does more than that. It disparages those who bring up race. Johnnie Cochran was said to have played the race card when he raised race as an issue in the Simpson trial. However, *Time* magazine was not accused of playing the race card when it intentionally darkened its cover mug-shot photograph of O.J. Simpson—a tactic designed to make him appear more Black, sinister and, alas, more guilty.

Such deflections are fairly transparent because those who use it are unable to state when race *is* a factor. Is it only a factor in Black-on-Black crimes or in Black-on-White crimes? If Tawana Brawley, and Al Sharpton as her representative, can be said to have played the race card, certainly the same can be said of Susan Smith—the White mother who fabricated an elaborate racial hoax to cover up the fact that she killed her two young boys.[29] In fact, it is hard to think of a case involving a Black man charged with a crime in America where race is not somehow involved, either overtly or covertly (particularly when we consider the relationship between race and income, education, and employment). Alleging that someone played the race card suggests that race has been introduced when it is irrelevant or nonexistent.

The charge of playing the race card is more a statement of how differently racial groups view the salience of race. Whites tend to think in terms of "colorlessness," while African Americans overwhelmingly believe that "race matters." Equally important, however, is the fact that the impact of race is rarely acknowledged in cases other than those involving Black offenders.

Is the Emperor Wearing Clothes?

Another cost of Black protectionism, as currently practiced, is that its broad-scale availability gives ammunition to those who question its legitimacy.[30] If Black protectionism is applied with equal fervor to cases as disparate as O.J. Simpson, Jesse Jackson, and Bill Clinton (who is not even Black!), it is fair to question its efficacy. The standardless use of Black protectionism raises the question of whether it is a reasonable form of Black resistance against racism or something much less. Is it a real strategy for racial justice or a façade? Hence, in cases where Black protectionism springs into action, it is fair to ask whether the emperor (Blacks in their exercise of protectionism) has on any clothes at all. Has there been a legitimate cry of racial foul in the case or does protectionism provide a mindless defense?

Conclusion

There is much about Black protectionism to recommend. At the same time, there are many valid criticisms as to how it works. These criticisms severely undercut Black protectionism's usefulness. It is now time to consider a new paradigm for applying protectionism. Based upon the above critique, the next chapter reconfigures Black protectionism so that it can operate as a workable civil rights strategy.

The way Black protectionism now works adds new meaning to the 1980s expression, popular on Black college campuses, "It's a Black thing, you wouldn't understand." It may be that those outside the Black community may not understand (or accept) Black protectionism. However, it should minimally make sense to those *within* the Black community. This chapter demonstrates the many weak points of Black protectionism, including its failure to sanction, its apolitical character, its failure to protect Black women, its promotion of blind race loyalty, and its promotion of the idea that Blacks are a monolithic group. Today's practice of Black protectionism is off track. It needs to be reenvisioned in a way that strengthens its core and acknowledges and corrects its weaknesses.

In chapter 6, I propose some new rules for racial protectionism. New guidelines are needed to impose some form of discipline upon the use of protectionism. The goal of these boundaries is to make the practice of Black protectionism both internally and externally consistent and coherent—and make it more likely to promote the goals of racial justice.

Black protectionism is an outsider's discourse. It is an attempt to address the social, economic, and political marginalization of African Americans. Although ostensibly intended to enhance racial justice, in its present form it does not. Specifically, it lacks a critical analysis of when protectionism is properly applied. Therefore, to be effective Black protectionism must be reformulated and given identifiable parameters. To promote the best interests of the Black community, Black protectionism must be reconstituted in a way that ensures that it works only to empower.

Declan Haun/Chicago Historical Society

CRITICAL BLACK PROTECTIONISM

Introduction

What would it take to make Black protectionism work properly? What has to be done to ensure that it promotes the goals of racial justice? Based on the discussion in the previous chapters, Black protectionism needs to be rethought and reworked if it is going to be effective. This chapter explores methods of reformulating protectionism so that it can meet its intended goals. What is needed is a *critical* application of Black protectionism. This chapter compares and contrasts the current system of Black protectionism with a restructured one. This multistage reformulation is labeled *critical Black protectionism*. As detailed, it keeps and expands the best practices of Black protectionism, while eliminating its weakest links. By using examples to detail how critical Black protectionism works, this chapter shows how Black protectionism operates differently from critical Black protectionism; how the Black community can best evaluate cases with Black offenders and Black victims; and how the new Black protectionism proposes to handle "repeat offenders."

Out with the Old, In with the New

A Critical Approach

The development of critical Black protectionism draws from critical race theory approaches to the law. In a nutshell, critical race theory is designed to challenge the conventional wisdom and social construction that people of color are deviant; to examine the law, its application, and its racial impact; and, ultimately, to reduce the ways in which the law and legal systems reinforce racial inequities. One novel aspect of critical race theory is that it incorporates narratives—stories told from the front lines of racial conflict. Ultimately, critical race theory offers the possibility of charting new courses to achieve racial justice.

On a smaller scale, critical Black protectionism has some features and goals in common with critical race theory. Specifically, the revised form of Black protectionism is designed to spotlight racial injustice perpetuated through the court system and to offer another tool to empower members of the African American community in the fight for racial justice. Importantly, critical Black protectionism also highlights, values, and incorporates the perspectives and voices of Black community members (see chapter 4).

Operating Mechanisms

In the current scheme, Black protectionism only arises in cases where there is an allegation of crime or unethical conduct against a well-known African American. As shown in table 6.1, however, critical Black protectionism expands the reach of protectionism—making it available in cases involving not only offenders, but victims as well. As important, the proposed model does not have a "celebrity" requirement. A nonfamous person who has been accused of a crime (e.g., Marcus Dixon[1]) or one who has been victimized by crime (e.g., Rodney King) may be eligible for Black protectionism.

Table 6.1. Operating Mechanisms for Black Protectionism, Current and Proposed

Current Operating Mechanisms	Proposed Operating Mechanisms
1. An allegation of wrongdoing	1. An allegation of wrongdoing or victimization
2. Against someone Black	2. By or against someone Black
3. By a mainstream agent	3. By a mainstream agent
4. (Against someone with a) national reputation or credibility as a racial spokesperson	

Additional Trigger Questions

Critical Black protectionism offers a new set of trigger questions for Blacks (see chapter 3). Table 6.2 contrasts the trigger questions for Black protectionism with those for critical Black protectionism. The new model adds two more questions for consideration. It considers what contributions the Black person who has been accused of a crime (or been a crime victim) has made to the Black community (question 7). The answer to this question necessitates an evaluation of not only *whether* but the *degree to which* the person accused (or victimized) has contributed to the community. Examples of community service include donating money to causes that address issues of particular concern in the Black community (e.g., sickle cell anemia research, the NAACP, the United Negro College Fund, antipoverty programs, and HIV/AIDS research) and speaking out on issues that acutely affect the Black community. Another factor to consider could be whether the potential recipient has embraced his Blackness or expressed pride in his racial heritage. In order to determine whether the answer to question 7 is "yes," the person's entire career as a public person should be considered. The goal is to make an assessment based on the totality of the person's "community service." Ultimately, this question assesses whether the person has paid his race dues.

Adding question 7 forces an evaluation of the specific Black person who would benefit from protectionism. In this way critical Black protectionism becomes a more thoughtful and reflective practice. This "race plus" analysis appropriately makes the Black community the focus of Black protectionism rather than the individual in trouble.

Question 8 emphasizes that critical Black protectionism should focus on the Black community. It asks whether it will help the community to rally behind the person who has been charged with an offense or been victimized by crime. This question pushes the community to engage in a sociopolitical calculus to determine whether it should offer Black protectionism. This assessment would be based on an array of factors, including the facts of the case (e.g., the seriousness of the crime), whether the case raises issues relevant to the African American community (locally or nationally), and the potential political benefits and costs of supporting the person. To determine this, community members have to determine how applying protectionism would affect Blacks as a group. Together questions

Table 6.2.   Revised Trigger Questions for Critical Black Protectionism

1. Did he commit the offense?

2. Even if he did was he set up?

3. Would he risk everything he has (e.g., wealth, fame, material possessions) to commit an offense?

4. Is he the only person who has committed the offense?

5. Do Whites accused of committing the same offense receive the same scrutiny and treatment?

6. Is the accusation part of a conspiracy to destroy the Black race?

ADDITIONAL QUESTIONS

7. Has the person done anything for the Black community (e.g., philanthropy, community service, been outspoken on community issues, expressed pride in being Black)?*

8. Is it in the Black community's best interest to provide support?

*This question is only relevant in cases involving a celebrity offender or victim.

7 and 8 move critical Black protectionism to an analysis that is more concerned with politics than personalities.

In many instances, there will be disagreement among community members as to whether a particular case warrants Black protectionism. Unanimity, however, is not what is important. What is important is that the new protectionism encourages analytical thought and reflection through the eyes of the community it serves. In fact, the additional trigger questions may move the community toward a broader consensus. Because critical Black protectionism allows room for what would have been dismissed as alternative or outside viewpoints (see chapter 5), its application in a particular case may appeal to a broader segment of African Americans.

With the addition of trigger questions 7 and 8, protectionism is treated as a privilege, not a right. You need something more than Black skin to receive Black protectionism. For example, in order for the community to show support for an unknown Black crime victim this support has to further the needs of the community. In cases involving well-known Blacks, in order for them to receive protection, they are required to have done something in order to get the benefit of Black protectionism.

Using past cases as a guide, the Black community favors celebrities. The rich and famous among us are more likely to be granted protectionism. It is in these cases, then, that the community has to be the most vigilant in deciding whether protectionism is appropriate. The same concern, however, does not exist in cases involving lesser-known African Americans. There may be a higher threshold for applying critical Black protectionism in these instances because the community is less likely to have a preexisting affiliation or strong allegiance to the person.

The revamped operating mechanisms and trigger questions radically alter the current practice of Black protectionism. Not only has the scope of Black protectionism been expanded, more is asked of the African American community. Critical Black protectionism requires active engagement—thought, discussion, assessment, and reflection. It is no longer a passive exercise. To work effectively and to protect those who might have fallen below the radar previously, the new protectionism encourages an engaged and aware African American community. This means that the community's attention and interest has to be focused on the famous and not-so-famous cases. The next section details the new processes, step by step, created by critical Black protectionism.

Critical Black Protectionism: A Road Map

Overview

Figure 6.1 outlines the three-part process for the newly formulated Black protectionism. In the first stage, as in its initial version, Black protectionism can be triggered by a charge against a well-known Black person. Critical Black protectionism expands its coverage to include nonfamous, everyday Blacks. In the second stage, the community's response to the allegations should focus on asserting the person's constitutional rights. At the same time, the community should openly acknowledge the problem of crime and victimization within the African American community. When it is evident from the facts, the community should criticize any inappropriate behavior (e.g., drug use, infidelity). The third stage, only available in some cases, arises when the community concludes that it should rally behind the person who has been charged with crime or been victimized by crime. In form and scope, the new Black protectionism works in a way that is dramatically distinct from the way Black protectionism currently operates. Critical Black protectionism is an informed and empowering application of race-based action designed to promote racial justice.

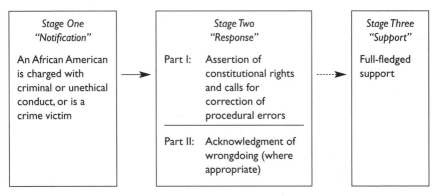

Figure 6.1. Stages of Critical Black Protectionism

Stage One ("Notification")

The first stage of critical Black protectionism is "notification." At this stage members of the public, including African Americans, receive information that someone Black has been accused of a crime or has been victimized by crime. Although the new protectionism applies to cases involving Black offenders and victims, it is likely that the cases most likely to receive it will be those involving Black celebrities who have been charged with crime. Cases involving Black crime victims have not garnered as much Black protectionism as other cases. The one exception has been cases involving police brutality. For instance, cases involving unarmed Black victims of police killings and beatings—e.g., Amadou Diallo, Abner Louima, and Rodney King—have received major press attention and support within the African American community.

It is hoped that critical Black protectionism will encourage the Black community to rally behind Black victims of police abuse, even though the issue of police brutality is no longer on the media's front burner. By way of example, in a June 2004 case of police abuse, members of the Los Angeles Police Department (LAPD) chased and beat an unarmed Black suspect. Following a car chase, officers sought to subdue the suspect, a thirty-six-year-old Black man. The videotaped incident shows one officer kicking and beating the man eleven times.[2] Likewise, in February 2005, the LAPD shot and killed Devin Brown, a thirteen-year-old Black boy. Brown was in the vehicle with another underaged youth who police said was driving in an erratic manner. Police opened fire and Brown was killed.

Although both cases received national publicity, neither case drew much response from the Black community outside of the Los Angeles area. In its pursuit of racial justice, the Black community can ill afford to ignore or shrug off well-publicized instances of police abuse.

Clearly, however, one goal of critical Black protectionism is for the Black community to "see" and protect victims beyond those subjected to police abuse. This would include extending the community's cloak of protection to a larger range of criminal cases, including victims of rape and murder, and those who have been wrongly convicted.

Critical Black protectionism also includes a category of cases involving accusations of ethical lapses or "inappropriate" action. Examples include the incidents involving Jesse Jackson, Lani Guinier, and Joycelyn Elders (see chapter 3). Although they do not involve allegations of criminal conduct, they remain important and deserve consideration for Black protectionism. As is true for criminal cases, these cases have the potential of derailing prominent African Americans from seeking or holding high-profile posts.

Stage Two ("Response")

The second stage has two parts. The first part acts as a check on the justice system. Specifically, it uses the media case under scrutiny to point out the continuing racial disparities within the justice system. The case in the media spotlight provides a platform for discussing how African Americans fare in the criminal justice system. Here the focus is on the process, not the person. Once a Black person (well-known or unknown) is charged with criminal or unethical conduct, the proposed protectionism calls for fair treatment.

For instance, in each case, members of the Black community would be outspoken in asserting the person's rights. The need to defend these rights would be highlighted by Blacks in their informal conversations (e.g., at the hairdresser or barber shop) as well as in conversations with members of the mainstream public (e.g., at work). The message that the person deserves fair treatment would be the same whether it was Jesse Jackson or Jimmy Jackson.

This response would send the unmistakable message that regardless of how the case is resolved, Blacks believe the person deserves a fair hearing and if the case is criminal, that he is entitled to the presumption of innocence. Given that the African American community already engages in this practice—standing up for the fallen Black person—this part of the response will not be difficult.

Because this part of the analysis focuses on how cases are handled, its sweep is broad. Importantly, Black protectionism in its new form does not favor the Black elite. It is instrumental: It demands fairness in highly publicized cases as a way of keeping the court system and the media honest. Black protectionism cannot extend support in every case where a Black person is alleged to have committed a crime—not even in all cases involving famous Blacks (see the appendix). That said, it is imperative that critical Black protectionism operate in nationally known cases—because incidents that receive widespread media attention serve as object lessons for the treatment that the Black community receives from the justice system.

Stage Two, Part II

The second part of Stage Two focuses on the crime (either what the person is accused of or the crime they were victimized by). Here the Black community shifts its focus away from how the person under scrutiny is being treated (e.g., how he is being portrayed by the press) to a focus on the allegations against the person. At this stage, the community evaluates the charges. For example, the community could decide to speak out against drug use or infidelity. Critical Black protectionism does not give a pass to the Black person under scrutiny, the victim, or the government. It acknowledges wrongdoing and calls for sanctions where appropriate. This component enables Black protectionism to more accurately reflect the moral sensibilities of the African American community. The importance of this stage cannot be overstated. Without it, the Black community sends a message that it does not take crime and violence seriously. Without it, in celebrity cases, the Black community sends a message that crimes of the rich and powerful should be accorded a different, exalted status. These would be odd and unfortunate messages to send given that African Americans are disproportionately more likely to be victims of violent crime than members of other racial groups.[3]

Stage Two: Applications

In this new scheme, how would Black protectionism work? In the Kobe Bryant case it would mean that the community would respond that he should not be railroaded by the justice system, was entitled to confront his accuser, and deserves the presumption of innocence. Critical Black protectionism also asserts that the crime of rape is a violent physical assault and is never justifiable or excusable. It also says that Bryant, a married man, used poor judgment in inviting an unknown woman to his hotel room. However, critical Black protectionism does *not* say that African Americans should blindly support Bryant because he is Black.

Applied to the Marion Barry case, the first part of the second stage allows two claims to be made. One claim is that the government took unprecedented steps to catch Barry using drugs. The concern for a fair and just process may raise numerous issues—for example, whether Barry was the victim of entrapment and selective prosecution, and whether the government used more resources to "set him up" than they used to get White politicians under scrutiny. Claim two is that smoking crack is wrong, whether done by a Black politician or anyone else. Drug use should not be excused by questionable government tactics.

Thus, critical Black protectionism allows for a bifurcated response. The criminal charges against Bryant and Barry (and others similarly situated) should be used as an opportunity to spotlight racial bias within the justice system. The charges can be used to assert the community's moral perspective—e.g., that rape, infidelity, and drug use are not condoned.

In the first and second stages, reconstituted Black protectionism treats African Americans in the same manner, regardless of their political affiliations. To the extent that critical Black protectionism is structured to promote procedural due process (Stage Two, Part I), all of the cases are treated the same. This is true without regard to the nature of the crime charged— from low-level drug use to murder.

In the Clarence Thomas case, once the sexual assault allegations were made against him, Black protectionism properly surfaced to ensure that the confirmation process would be fair. At this stage, critical Black protectionism is focused on how the person under scrutiny is treated by the court system or government and seeks to make sure that his rights are protected. This includes a look at whether the legal process has been fair (e.g., was he read his rights, did he have access to an attorney?). This also includes a look at how the person is treated by the press (e.g., whether the person was treated as though he had the presumption of innocence).

Together, the first and second parts of Stage Two allow Black protectionism to make a statement—whenever someone has been charged with a crime, there may be more than one victim. Of course, there is the person who says they were victimized. However, there is also another potential victim, the person who is charged with the crime. They may have been falsely accused of crime and railroaded through the system, partly due to their race. The remaining question, addressed in the next section, is what role politics should play in determining whether the Black community should do more than argue for due process in a particular case.

Stage Three ("Support")

The third stage of critical Black protectionism is the "support" component. After there have been checks on procedural fairness, and comment on the wisdom of the offender's (or victim's) actions, there must be a critical review of whether *any* further community action is warranted. As indicated by the dotted border in figure 6.1, Stage Three will not always operate. In fact, it should not go into effect in most cases. At this stage the community should ask whether it should use any more of its racial capital to actively defend the person who has been charged (or who is alleging victimization). It is here that trigger question 8 ("Is it in the Black community's best interest to provide support?") is applied. A few additional questions—subquestions—should be asked in order to determine whether the answer to question 8 is yes or no. These include:

i) Which type of offense is involved?

ii) Will the community receive (or lose) any tangible benefits if it offers support?

iii) Will the community receive (or lose) any intangible benefits if it offers support?

iv) Will community support for the person make a clear statement about racial injustice in the U.S. court system?

Answering these questions requires an examination of the cost and value of offering Black protectionism.

To answer the first subquestion, the community would take into consideration the type of crime or infraction involved in the case. For instance, it would look at whether the case involves a felony (e.g., murder), misdemeanor (e.g., drug use), or something less serious (e.g., adultery, parenting a child outside of marriage). Thus, it makes sense that the community would differentiate between the cases involving Jesse Jackson (adultery) and Rae Carruth (murder).

For the second question, the community would determine whether support for the person would yield any long-term benefits to the community (regardless of the case outcome). In the case of a celebrity charged with a crime, if the community provides support, is that person likely to engage in or continue philanthropic activities beneficial to the community? On the flip side, will the denial of support from the community mean that the celebrity will withdraw their financial support from the community? A serious consideration of this question in the O.J. Simpson case would likely have reduced the amount of support he garnered from the Black community.

Even if no tangible benefits are at issue, the community should determine whether there are other reasons to provide or deny Black protectionism (subquestion iii). For instance, the community might consider what, if any, White backlash will result from its decision to support the person. Again the Simpson case is an object lesson. Ideally the Black community would have critically evaluated whether supporting Simpson at all costs would be worth it in the long run. In supporting him, were the benefits to the community greater than the costs of denying him Black protectionism? The issue of White backlash, however, should *not* be a deciding factor, but rather a consideration that is weighed against the reasons for granting Black protectionism.

The fourth subquestion focuses on cases that highlight racial discrimination within the justice system. These cases are most likely to involve noncelebrities. This category includes incidents of police brutality. It also covers racial profiling, referred to as "Driving while Black." Examples include two cases brought in the 1990s by targets of racial profiling against the Maryland State Troopers and the New Jersey State Troopers. Cases involving low-level offenders who face extremely harsh penalties under mandatory minimum-sentencing schemes also highlight racial bias within the system. The case of Kemba Smith, a drug courier who transported crack cocaine for her abusive, drug-dealing boyfriend, exemplifies this. For her minor role as a drug mule, Smith, a college student, was sentenced to twenty-four years in federal prison. Smith served more than six years behind bars before being pardoned by President Bill Clinton in 2001. Other examples include cases involving inmates who have been exonerated based upon DNA evidence (including many on death row).[4]

The third stage ("support") erects a high threshold for applying critical Black protectionism. It requires a consideration of many factors to determine whether Black protectionism is warranted in a particular case. This analysis is a long way from the knee-jerk reaction that characterizes "old" Black protectionism. The African American community will not always agree on how each case should be handled, regarding a grant of Black protectionism. What is valuable about the proposed approach, however, is that it offers a thoughtful method for reviewing these cases—an approach that takes into consideration politics, history, law, and sociology. Because critical Black protectionism goes beyond the facts of a particular case involving a prominent Black person charged with crime, it is a step forward.

Together the three stages of critical Black protectionism offer a road map for Black community action in cases involving a well-known Black charged with or victimized by crime, or in those cases involving a crime charged or an injustice committed against an average Black person. It addresses several of the weaknesses of Black protectionism (see chapter 5). First, by requiring a case-by-case analysis, it avoids the traps of blind race loyalty. Second, by expanding protection to include noncelebrities, it does not have a built-in celebrity bias, which is inherent in the current practice of Black protectionism. Third, by making a distinction between "response" and "support," critical Black protectionism imposes a political framework around the exercise of Black protectionism—moving it from apolitical to political. Fourth, it rejects the Black monolith myth by expanding the groups that can receive shelter under the umbrella of Black protectionism (celebrities and noncelebrities; victims and offenders). This expanded focus also encourages the embrace of Black women—a group that has been largely overlooked—as deserving of Black protectionism. Finally, the three-stage model addresses the need for accountability and sanctions by drastically winnowing down the number of people who are eligible for protectionism.

Critical Black Protectionism: O.J. and Jesse

This section revisits two well-known cases involving Black protectionism, those of O.J. Simpson and Jesse Jackson. It looks at how differently the

Black community would have responded to these cases had it applied critical Black protectionism.

O.J., Again

Would the Black community's response to the O.J. Simpson case have been any different if it had applied a critical Black protectionism approach? In Stage One of critical Black protectionism there is notification—the community becomes aware that someone Black has been charged with a crime, been the victim of a crime, or been accused of some ethical misstep. Under the old scheme, the only people who are eligible for protectionism are well-known Blacks. Under either system, Simpson, who was charged with double murder, would make it past the initial barrier of eligibility for Black protectionism.

The second stage, or response, calls for the involvement of the Black community. Now that they know about the criminal charges, the community's next step in protecting one of its own is to make sure that the person under scrutiny, Simpson, receives fair treatment. At this point, members of the community should be vocal about the need to ensure that the accused person's constitutional rights are protected. For Simpson that would mean that he had counsel, that he is not presumed guilty and thereby railroaded through the system. During this stage, community members could also evaluate the police's consideration of other reasonable theories of the crime and the possibility of other suspects. In Simpson's case, his all-star attorneys made sure that his basic legal guarantees were protected.

Many African Americans, however, openly expressed concern that Simpson was being railroaded because Whites did not like the fact that his second wife was a young White, blonde woman. All responses tied to substantive and procedural justice are appropriate in the first part of Stage Two. Therefore, when well into the criminal trial a tape-recorded interview revealed that LA police detective and key prosecution witness Mark Fuhrman had used the "N word" numerous times (he initially denied using the slur), Blacks rightfully questioned his credibility and the strength of the prosecution's case. This stage is not explicitly a part of the earlier version of Black protectionism. However, the assertion of rights and protections form the core of Black protectionism.

Applying critical Black protectionism also means that the Black community has to, where appropriate, acknowledge wrongdoing. In the Simpson case that would have meant acknowledging the harms of domestic violence. It would also have meant acknowledging that if Simpson did commit the murders that he should receive the appropriate punishment. We heard very little of this sentiment expressed openly by members of the African American community. In part this reflects the community's reluctance to consider alternative viewpoints. Much of the focus was on defending Simpson and protecting him against what many believed were false charges. This new requirement for Black protectionism is an important addition. It signals that the practice of protectionism would no longer be an automatic response by community members. It also signals that community members believe that Blacks and Whites alike should be accountable for their actions. Sending this message is particularly important since African Americans are disproportionately affected by violent crime.

The third stage of critical Black protectionism represents the most significant departure for Black protectionism. In its new form, critical Black protectionism allows the African American community to provide support, active support, for *some* of the people who are eligible for Black protectionism. The cloak of racial support is no longer given as a free pass to any famous Black person who finds himself in legal hot water. In the Simpson case, the community rallied behind him from the time the murder charges were filed through the acquittal. He received vocal and visible community support. If critical Black protectionism were applied, however, the community's response would have looked very different. African Americans as a group should have weighed and balanced more thoughtfully whether to give full community support to Simpson. This would have included a consideration of his ties to the community—his direct involvement, charitable donations, and more generally his identification with Blacks. Based on this, community members could have reasonably concluded that it would receive little in return (tangible or otherwise) for offering protectionism to O.J.

Jesse Jackson

By way of comparison, it is worth examining how the proposed Black protectionism would apply to the case involving Jesse Jackson. In 2001, Jackson was accused of adultery and fathering a child out of wedlock with a mistress. Both the type of offense (ethical) and Jackson's involvement with the Black community present a different set of issues from those raised in the Simpson case.

As always, during the first stage, the community learns that someone Black has been accused of a crime or an ethical lapse. As noted, applying "old" Black protectionism means that the accused has to be someone famous. Using either "old" or "new" Black protectionism, however, Jackson's case is eligible for Black protectionism.

In the second stage the community makes its voice heard. Once the rumor surfaced that Jackson had an out-of-wedlock child, many African Americans voiced concern as to why this was a national story. In particular, questions were raised as to whether Jackson was being subject to heightened scrutiny because of his race and because of his liberal politics. Notably, the rumors surfaced just as Jackson was planning a rally in Tallahassee, Florida, to protest the voting irregularities in the 2000 presidential election. Applying critical Black protectionism during the second stage (Part I), it is appropriate for community members to express suspicions and doubts and insist on fair and equitable treatment. For instance, the community was right in demanding that the media not apply a double standard to Jackson's case: If his case merits wide-scale publicity so do all other cases involving similarly situated politicians and community advocates.

After calling for fairness, however, critical Black protectionism imposes a responsibility on community members to speak out about the particular crime or ethical offense (without assuming guilt). In Jackson's case that would have meant at least weighing in on adultery—that an extramarital affair, although not unlawful, raises moral concerns. Many members of the Black community appeared reluctant to say anything negative about Jackson, a revered reverend and civil rights leader. Commentators on the conservative right, however, did not bite their tongues. The Black community would not have lost any clout by publicly acknowledging that adultery is wrong. Critical Black protectionism encourages community members to speak out against offenses (criminal and ethical) that cause harm to its members (Stage Two, Part II). There is no contradiction in arguing that the accused has constitutional rights that must be protected *and* insisting on accountability for group members who engage in offenses.

Jackson's case, however, took an unusual turn. Not long after the published allegations, Jackson admitted to having an affair and admitted to fathering a child out of wedlock. He took full responsibility for his actions and stated that he was paying child support. Given this, it should have been easy for community members to criticize his actions since Jackson himself acknowledged the harm his actions caused his family. These facts make this case unlike most others where someone is accused of something and they adamantly deny the charges.

The third stage focuses on the degree of support the community should give to the person accused of wrongdoing (or victimized by crime). To determine this, the community has several factors to consider, including the type of offense involved (e.g., seriousness), the benefit to the community of providing protection, whether support will advance the cause of racial justice, and the person's commitment to the Black community. In Jackson's case, an evaluation of these considerations points to granting Black protectionism—especially when compared with Simpson.

First, Jackson's actions involved issues of morality, not criminality. Saying this does not diminish the harms caused by his actions, rather it puts those harms in perspective—e.g., comparing it with other, more serious, offenses, such as murder or rape. As well, in considering Jackson's ethical lapse, the community could reasonably take into account his role as a respected religious leader and activist for civil rights. Second, there is a clear benefit to the community in protecting one of its members who has stood and fought for racial justice. Even for those who might question Jackson's strategies and tactics regarding how to best achieve a racially just society (e.g., focus on corporate diversity), his commitment to the Black community is long-standing. Further, if the person is removed from the community (e.g., imprisoned), the community loses a valued member. Related to this, standing up for Jackson's civil rights work while at the same time criticizing his wrongdoing promotes the overall goals of racial justice.

In a poll taken during the Jackson episode, 64 percent of the Blacks surveyed had a "favorable" opinion of him, compared with 24 percent of the Whites surveyed. This indicates that Jackson received a much lower level of support from the community than Simpson. Given their different allegiances and level of involvement in the Black community, had critical Black protectionism been applied, the Black community's support for Simpson would have been lukewarm compared with its support for Jackson. In both cases, however, community members should have argued for protecting both men's constitutional guarantees (e.g., privacy, presumption of innocence).

When Offenders and Victims Collide:
Competing Allegiances?

In some instances, members of the community will be faced with choosing between an offender and a victim. The bottom line question is whether it serves the community's best interests to protect the person in question. The case involving Mike Tyson and Desiree Washington provides a useful example of this situation.

In the Tyson case, lines in the sand were drawn early on. After hearing about the charges against Tyson, much of the Black community quickly and overwhelmingly sided with him, offering its support. Tyson, a well-known and well-liked prizefighter, had been popular for more than a decade. When he was accused of raping Desiree Washington, a young, then unknown, beauty pageant contestant, many dismissed the charges as at best a private misunderstanding or at worst a gold-digging scheme. In boxing terms, Tyson's popularity, celebrity status, and the nature of the criminal charge combined to affect a TKO—landing Washington on the canvas.

Conversations about the case at Black places of business (e.g., hair salons, barbershops, bars, and restaurants) centered on various rhetorical questions including why would Tyson, who is young, rich, and famous, have to "take it?" According to this perspective, rich people are incapable of committing a sex crime. Discussion about the case also focused on whether the charges were part of a larger plan (see trigger question 6: "Is the accusation part of a conspiracy to destroy the Black race?"). Followed to their logical conclusions, both of these perspectives would conclusively presume that any celebrity defendant who has been charged with a crime is "innocent." This is a far cry from the presumption of innocence.

Under the proposed scheme for new Black protectionism, how would the Black community have responded to the Tyson case? Whether Black protectionism or critical Black protectionism is being applied, the notification stage remains the same. During this phase the Black community learns that one of its members, famous or common, has been charged with a crime (or been the victim of a crime). The first part of the response stage, involving the assertion of constitutional rights, is also a feature of old and new Black protectionism. Accordingly, the Black community did and should have (per critical Black protectionism) insisted that Tyson was entitled to the same constitutional protections as everyone else, including the presumption of innocence and the right to a fair trial. Further, that the media and the public should not rush to judgment.

However, as we move to Stage Two (Part II) the differences between critical Black protectionism and "old" Black protectionism become apparent. During this stage the Black community would have acknowledged Desiree Washington as the victim in the Tyson case and publicly acknowledged the impact of sexual assault on members of the community. Having quickly dismissed her claims as unbelievable, Washington was excoriated. While there was no rush to judge Tyson, there was a rush to judge Washington. The charges, however, presented the community with an opportunity to discuss sexual assault—e.g., what it is, how prevalent it is, how to prevent it, and where victims can go for support. Instead, many African Americans did nothing more than staunchly defend Tyson. As a community, we were able to see the potential harms the charges would cause Tyson (and others similarly situated). At the same time, by failing to discuss them, the community made invisible the potential harms of sexual assault to Desiree Washington (and others similarly situated).

During the third stage of critical Black protectionism, the Black community considers whether to go the extra mile in supporting the Black person in trouble with the law or the press. In the Tyson case there were many factors to consider. On the plus side, Tyson was well liked and closely linked to the Black community. He views himself as a Black man and has embraced the Black community. His hardscrabble beginnings, including early scrapes with the law, made him a sympathetic figure. Tyson has also been known to give generously to causes that help minorities and the underprivileged. On the negative side, Tyson's temper and penchant for rogue behavior has been well documented. In addition to allegations of domestic assault, Tyson has been referred to as a "serial buttocks fondler." On balance, it is understandable that community members felt some allegiance with Tyson.

It remains questionable, however, whether all the stops should have been pulled out in supporting Tyson, especially when it meant leaving another community member, Washington, in the lurch. Given the rates of victimization, the community does not win anything by championing offenders and marginalizing victims. As noted earlier, there is a long history of ignoring crimes of sexual assault crimes perpetrated against African American females. The question should be asked, who "needs" protection more, a twenty-five-year-old man or an eighteen-year-old woman? In the case of R. Kelly, who needs protection more, a thirty-four-year-old man or a thirteen-year-old girl?

The Clarence Thomas case raised issues similar to the Tyson case. Here also Blacks were faced with deciding between the stories of two high-profile Blacks. Here the community missed an opportunity to educate others and learn about the prevalence of sexual assault, its harms, and its remedies (Stage Two, Part II). The community's primary focus during the Thomas hearings was on how it looked like Whites were trying to bring another Black man down—a view only enhanced by the televised all-White, all-male Senate committee that grilled Thomas on his sexual proclivities.

Unlike Tyson, however, the argument for supporting Thomas was much weaker (Stage Three). There is little in Thomas's preconfirmation record that would identify him as supportive of or identifying with the Black community. Thomas had positioned himself as a conservative's conservative (e.g., anti–affirmative action and anti–civil rights programs), and he took pains to distinguish himself from the average Black person. Thomas's up from poverty story, however, did resonate with many African Americans—many assuming that once he made it onto the Supreme Court, his roots would be a constant reminder and would push him to stand for the poor and oppressed. At the time of Thomas's nomination, there was little tangible basis for providing community support. Further, the larger Black community has not benefited from his seat on the Supreme Court in the intervening fifteen years. The community's support for Thomas only helped to ensure that there would remain a Black person on the Court. An internally consistent approach to Black protectionism—such as the proposed critical Black protectionism—would question *any* Supreme Court nominee (Black or White) who is opposed to civil rights advances and struggles.

It is notable that both the Tyson and Thomas cases involve claims of sexual assault. This is a hot button issue for Black protectionism. African Americans are particularly sensitive to allegations of sex crimes against Black men. These claims are likely to raise suspicions when the victim is White (e.g., Kobe Bryant case). This nation's history is riddled with stories of Black men being strung up and lynched, imprisoned, or run out of town based on the claims of White women (see chapter 2). This history has led to community reluctance to support rape victims, particularly those claiming "date rape." It has also led to community reluctance to believe White women who claim to have been assaulted by Black men (e.g., O.J. Simpson). This raises the question: Should the exercise of Black protectionism allow the community to favor a Black man charged with raping a White woman—given this country's history of lynching and racial hoaxes?[5] Critical Black protectionism answers "no"—and challenges community members to decide each case by the facts at hand.

All told, rejecting the view that offenders are competing with victims allows for a nuanced application of protectionism. Critical Black protectionism eliminates the perceived problem of warring racial allegiances. It does not pit Mike Tyson against Desiree Washington, Clarence Thomas against Anita Hill, or Bill Clinton against Joycelyn Elders. It holds that Mike Tyson *and* Desiree Washington, Clarence Thomas *and* Anita Hill, and Bill Clinton *and* Joycelyn Elders deserve due process. The African American community cannot afford to overlook how victims are treated within the justice system. The community is harmed when any member is mistreated or victimized by crime. Those who say they have been victimized by crime deserve their day in court, too. Further, the new Black protectionism allows protectionism to embrace women as well as men—an approach that is in the best interests of the community. Considering that Black women have been largely unable to tap into the Black protectionism well, this is an important feature of critical Black protectionism.

"Repeat Offenders"

Another category of cases that are eligible for Black protectionism but do not fit neatly into discussions of Black protectionism are those involving repeat, usually low-level offenders. There are some people who are routinely in trouble with the law. High-profile examples from the African American community include married couple Whitney Houston and Bobby Brown. Both have had several run-ins with the law, including Houston's rear-ending of a city bus and another incident in which she attempted to board a plane with marijuana. Brown has faced charges of drunk driving, lewd behavior, cocaine use, and domestic assault. Clearly Brown's offenses are more serious than Houston's. James Brown, as well, has had numerous brushes with the law, including charges for assault and battery. Notably, the allegations against Bobby Brown and James Brown are much more serious than those Whitney Houston has faced. These types of cases raise the issue of how the Black community should deal with repeat offenders. Specifically, applying the new protectionism, are they entitled to a community "response" or "support"?

The community appears to treat these cases the same way that they treat criminal cases involving rappers and athletes—with a yawning indifference (see chapter 3). With these celebrities there is little attempt to rally around them or to defend them. The tacit assumption seems to be that because of the person's prior bad behavior, it is likely that he did what he has been accused of doing. More than anything, these cases appear to provide material for jokes. Should *any* protectionism be available in these cases? Yes. Given that the operating principle behind critical Black protectionism is racial equity and fairness, then these cases are minimally entitled to a response (Stage Two, Part I).

Conclusion

Critical Black protectionism imposes an order and logic on "old" Black protectionism. It demands political consistency. While it acknowledges varied political viewpoints within the Black community, it always supports views that are in the group's best interest. A critical application of Black protectionism does not automatically label and dismiss criminal charges against a well-known African American as simply "a plot to destroy the Black man." The new Black protectionism allows the African American response to vary according to both the circumstances of the case and the person under scrutiny. It is neither a blanket denial of offending nor a wholesale racial embrace. Further, as reconfigured, it avoids the downsides associated with the current application of Black protectionism (see chapter 5). It does not excuse or minimize criminal behavior. As well, it offers a verbal sanction where appropriate (Stage Two, Part II). Also, unlike "old" Black protectionism, new Black protectionism does not shy away from political considerations—it encourages a political analysis in each case to determine whether it is worthy of a grant of protectionism. By definition, it opposes blind race loyalty.

The "new" protectionism is an affirmative action that African Americans can practice in response to race-based treatment. Over time, Blacks have had a uniquely negative experience with the justice system. The group's vantage point can operate as a check on whether the rights of the Black elite have been respected. Critical Black protectionism is a widely embraceable form of social protest.[6] It is a method of civil rights struggle that the masses of African Americans can engage in. It also acts as a bold affront to the dismissive, routine, and rhetorical query regarding how much better things are today for African Americans—a query that implies that Black racial progress somehow occurred in the absence of struggle. In this way, the revised Black protectionism offers what Patricia Williams calls a "political mechanism that can confront the *denial* of need."[7] At its best, Black protectionism operates as both a call to action and as a national history lesson.

Critical Black protectionism mandates a more active Black community. It offers a reenergized method of tackling and addressing some forms of racial inequity. Together the three stages, notice, response, and support, push Black protectionism beyond its previous confines. Critical Black protectionism requires that the Black community expand its base of interest in the criminal justice system, beyond well-known names and figures, to include not only everyday Blacks but also Black victims of crime. Critical Black protectionism recognizes that offenders and victims are entitled to have their cases heard and processed fairly through the justice system. It challenges community members to be circumspect in their decision to grant protection to members who find themselves in trouble with the law. In particular, the third stage serves as a buffer preventing a love-fest for famous, fallen community members. The new protectionism argues that the community does not benefit when "protecting our own" means protecting only the rich and famous within the group. The larger community gains when every member is valued and accorded the same protections, regardless of their fame or fortune. Critical Black protectionism also sends a clear message that racial justice is for the community at large, not select individuals who have "made it."

Walter Dean Myers

CHAPTER SEVEN
CONCLUDING THOUGHTS, NEW DIRECTIONS

Introduction

Thus far this book has tilled the basic ground of Black protectionism—its form, structure, and application. What remains to be done is to consider some of the secondary and tertiary issues associated with the phenomenon. This chapter identifies several issues that impact the expanse and effectiveness of Black protectionism. The first section considers whether non-Blacks should be encouraged to engage in Black protectionism. The second part follows up on the issue of whether protectionism should be available to non-Blacks, an issue broached earlier in the book. The third section considers the role of the media in enhancing or impeding the workability of protectionism. The fourth part focuses on the role of Black leadership in the success of applying critical Black protectionism. The final part considers the overall impact of protectionism and why protectionism matters. Each of these issues is considered in light of the overall discussion of Black protectionism.

Can Anyone Be a Black Protectionist?

Any person of any race or ethnicity can practice Black protectionism. There is no special race pass that limits protectionism to African Americans. The question posed here, however, asks whether members of other racial groups should be encouraged to engage in Black protectionism. Should African Americans actively solicit the support of others outside the community? And assuming non-Blacks can participate in critical Black protectionism, can they take part in all three stages? (see chapter 6)

In the fight for racial equality, there is a long history of multiracial coalitions working together. In the abolition movement, for example, Blacks and Whites fought together and separately to bring an end to U.S. chattel slavery. During the civil rights struggles of the 1950s and 1960s, diverse groups of African Americans, Whites, Latinos, Asians, American Indians, Christians, Jews, gays, Quakers, and students, joined forces to end racial segregation in public accommodations. Clearly Blacks are not the only group, racial or otherwise, concerned with ending racial discrimination.

However, enlisting the help of other groups in the campaign for Black protectionism may not be so easy. First, for those outside the community, the heightened role that celebrities play in Black life may be hard to understand. It may also be difficult for outsiders, particularly Whites, to comprehend the degree of systemic racial bias in the media. Their different life experiences present a challenge to expanding the pool of Black protectionists. It is uncertain whether members of other racial groups will see themselves as having a stake or interest in engaging in protectionism.

The Simpson case offers a lens through which to examine how Whites who would engage in Black protectionism would respond. Because it was so polarizing, the case presents some obvious challenges. For instance, helping more Whites understand that the Simpson case did involve issues of race and racism, at its core, would be difficult. Let us be clear, engaging in protectionism does *not* mean that Whites (or other non-Blacks) would have to believe that Simpson was innocent—especially since many African Americans did not think he was innocent. It would mean, however, that they would have minimally supported and encouraged the protection of his constitutional rights. Further, to apply protectionism in that case would indicate a willingness to challenge the media's biased representations in the case, including a darkened *Time* magazine cover photograph of Simpson. It would also require being open to alternative narratives about the case. When trial evidence surfaced that raised serious doubts about the credibility of prosecution witnesses it could not be ignored or dismissed.

Luckily the Simpson case does not represent the average Black protectionism case. It should be easier for members of other groups to be Black protectionists in cases that are not as racially-charged as the Simpson criminal trial. Also, Whites may be more willing to engage in protectionism where both the offender and victim are Black (e.g., Mike Tyson). In these cases they may be less sympathetic (and less subjective) toward a Black victim than they would a White victim. There were few polls during the Simpson case that examined the perspectives of other racial groups besides Blacks or Whites. This makes it difficult to know whether Latinos or Asians, for example, were more or less sympathetic toward Simpson.

A strong case can be made that other racial groups should be encouraged to practice Black protectionism. If members of other groups can see the need to participate in Black protectionism this will signal a big step toward cross-racial understanding of the nuances of race and racism. It is relatively easy to acknowledge the harm and moral wrongs of legally-imposed racial segregation. However, seeing the need for Black protectionism may be less apparent. Understanding the phenomenon of Black protectionism requires some knowledge of the history of race and racism in the United States. Specifically, it requires being able to analyze how this legal, social, and political history have affected and shaped the African American community. And, as important is how it has shaped White consciousness (e.g., the development and entrenchment of White privilege) and affected relationships between Blacks and other groups of color.

Benefit to the Community

Even if Whites and members of other racial groups are willing to practice Black protectionism, is this something that African Americans should embrace? Are there any advantages to keeping Black protectionism "in house"? Should it be guarded as an exercise in self-determination?

On the plus side, there are obvious benefits to having members of other groups engage in Black protectionism. One, it will mean that at least some people outside of the Black community agree that there is a need to protect the rights of Blacks who have been charged with crime and those victimized by crime. Two, it will mean that the Black community has a louder voice in the fight against racial discrimination. Three, inviting other groups to adopt protectionism continues the practice of earlier generations—using a broad-based coalition of support in the fight for racial justice and civil rights.

On the other side, if those outside the African American community are encouraged to be Black protectionists then others, outside the community, will have a say in what is "right" or "wrong" for the community.

Strategies for resolving this issue have to be considered before non-Blacks can be invited to add their voices to calls for Black protectionism.

Measuring "Help"

An inherent problem with Black protectionism is the difficulty of measuring support. Specifically, attempting to figure out how many people engage in the practice. Unless a case has attracted national attention, it is unlikely that there will be reliable polls or surveys taken to assess how Blacks or Whites view a particular case. Other indications of support must be used. Black media outlets are one resource for tracking responses by the African American community. This includes Black newspapers and magazines geared toward Black audiences and related websites. Even in those cases that attract large-scale attention, national poll data are not always divided by race. It is more likely that there will be a poll conducted that does not gather data on race (e.g., the daily CNN poll).

For instance, following the rape allegations against Kobe Bryant, there were few polls taken that included a racial breakdown (e.g., Black respondents versus White respondents). Several surveys, however, looked at whether the public was behind Bryant or believed he was guilty of the charges. In some instances, then, it will be easier to gauge the degree of broad, cross-racial support there is in a particular case. All of this means that it will be difficult to tell how many Blacks and non-Blacks have engaged in protectionism. Not only are these numbers not likely to be captured by polls, currently there is no main channel through which this information can be gathered.

Reporting for Duty

What exactly are the responsibilities of a non-Black Black protectionist? First, where along the continuum of critical Black protectionism do they fit in? The most logical fit is the "response" stage (see chapter 6). At this point, those applying Black protectionism voice their concerns about the accused or the victim. Specifically, the person is entitled to have his procedural rights protected and that the media should not prejudge the case outcome. Given the sensitivity of race relations, it is probably advisable that only Blacks (at least initially) participate in the second part of the response stage. In this part, the community, where appropriate, criticizes the person for wrongdoing and stresses the community's concern with addressing crime and violence. Also, the critical Black protectionist (of any race) can give protection to famous Blacks and those who are not well known.

All Aboard the Protectionism Train

The question of whether protectionism should be extended to protect Bill Clinton in particular and Whites in general, was raised in earlier chapters (see chapters 5 and 6). The issue here, however, is a broader one—whether Black protectionism should be available to members of other racial groups (not just Whites). For example, should Blacks extend protectionism to well-known Latinos, American Indians, Asians, and Whites, who find themselves in trouble with the law? If protectionism is available to non-famous Blacks, should it also be available to people of other races who are not famous? This section examines the issues associated with extending the reach of Black protectionism to non-Blacks, the costs, and the benefits.

Protecting Whites

Given that Black protectionism is a direct, ongoing response to White oppression, it will be difficult to make the case for extending it to Whites. Related to this, as one focus group member observed, Whites are protected by "White privilege" (see chapter 4). As members of the largest racial group in the United States and the group that holds the economic, political, and social power, Whites continually benefit from their skin color. In the criminal justice system, for instance, their Whiteness works for them, not against them. In the court of public opinion, Whites are more likely to be viewed as and treated as innocent until proven guilty. They are also more likely than Blacks to have financial resources to protect their procedural rights. Together, these facts arguably negate the need to use Black protectionism to benefit Whites.

Should there be any exceptions—circumstances in which Black protectionism is extended to Whites? What about a situation where a high-profile White person, one who has been an ally to the Black community, faces serious charges? This was the issue raised by the Clinton impeachment hearings. Again, the issue is whether the Black community's voice is *needed*—in the same way that it would be needed if the accused person were an African American. It also has to be determined whether there is some benefit to the African American community in providing a cloak of protection to Whites.

If protectionism is not given to well-known Whites who have been supportive of the Black community, should that also mean it will be denied to less well-known Whites? In many communities there are Whites who are involved in grass roots efforts that benefit communities of color. If one of these Whites was charged with a crime, should Black protectionism kick in? A strong argument can be made that anyone who works to enhance and improve conditions for Blacks should at least be considered for Black protectionism. Following this, if the ultimate goal of protectionism is to achieve racial justice, then those who are working toward this goal should benefit from protectionism. At the same time, however, the issue of White privilege exists for all Whites, not just those who are well known or famous.

Using the above standard, few instances involving White politicians or celebrities would trigger Black protectionism. The Clinton case stands out as an exception. At the national level it is difficult to come up with even a short list of names of Whites who are viewed as allies of the Black community—those who could generate wide-scale support within the community if they were in legal or ethical trouble. This reality may be the most important revelation from this discussion—that in the year 2005 there is little need to consider extending Black protectionism to Whites. Although there are Whites who work for racial justice, there are relatively few who are known throughout the Black community as engaged in this struggle.

Protecting Other People of Color

Given historical and contemporary realities, African Americans and other people of color share many common experiences. The argument for extending protectionism to other people of color, then, is more compelling than for granting it to Whites. There are, however, relatively few cases involving high-profile Latinos, Asian Americans, or American Indians that have called out for protectionism.

If we look beyond celebrity cases there are others to consider. Notably, one of the recent instances of ethnic protectionism—Elian Gonzalez—did not involve a famous person (see chapter 1). Other potential cases include police brutality incidents. There are legions of police assault incidents involving Latinos. Also, racial profiling cases often involve Latinos, Asian Americans, and American Indians.

In the wake of the September 2001 terrorist attacks, there has been a sharp rise in the number cases involving the profiling of Muslims in the United States. Hate crimes are another offense where the victims are often people of color. One of the more well-known cases involved Vincent Chin. In 1979, Chin, a Chinese American, who lived in Detroit, was killed. He was murdered by two laid-off White auto workers. The men believed that Chin was Japanese and that he somehow embodied the threat of American jobs lost to the wave of Japanese automobile imports.

There are very few cases of well-known people of color (beyond Blacks) that would invoke Black protectionism. Yet, there are numerous crime victims who could benefit from protection. In addition to cases involving racial profiling, police brutality, and hate crime, there are minorities who work for racial equality who could also use Black protectionism.

Assuming Black protectionism is available to non-Blacks, how much is enough? Are they entitled to both "response" and "support"? (see chapter 6). Does the answer to this depend upon whether the person is White or of color? If protectionism in the form of response is available, this means that African Americans would simply support the person's basic rights (e.g., fair trial). Again this raises the question of whether a response by the African American community is necessary—will it affect the outcome of a case, will it make a difference either symbolically or politically? If, extending protectionism to members of other groups includes support, then, the person would receive the full protection of the Black community.

Benefits and Costs

Based on the above discussion, it is clear that there are reasons to grant and deny Black protectionism to members of other racial groups. On the plus side, granting protectionism is an acknowledgment that the African American community is not a closed group. It is a statement that the community is not alone in its fight against racism. It is also an acknowledgement of the power of the Black community—that has a public voice that can help others, not just Blacks.

There are potential costs to making Black protectionism available to everyone. This raises a basic issue—is giving Black protectionism to Whites antithetical to very idea of *Black* protectionism? Assuming that it is workable, is it something that should be done? Arguably it is no longer Black protectionism if it is available without regard to race: It is protectionism. As noted, the existence of White privilege may moot the need or value of applying Black protectionism to Whites. Applying it to Whites, then, could only have a symbolic value. Further, the goals and implementation of Black protectionism may be minimized if its application is too broad.

Based on the above discussion, more thinking is required to determine whether Black protectionism should be limited to Blacks, should be extended to other groups of color, or should be available to everyone, including Whites. Before this decision is made, however, it is clear that it should first be established that critical Black protectionism is properly and consistently applied to African Americans. This is no small task. The community has to rework Black protectionism so that it is no longer a free, indiscriminate offering to any Black person with status. This includes an assessment of one's political involvement and his ties to the Black community.

At this time, Black protectionism should not be extended beyond the African American community. Before it is applied to members of other racial groups, it needs to be well established that critical Black protectionism works for African Americans before the practice is applied to other groups. To expand protectionism beyond the Black community without first establishing its workability within the community is potentially distracting and possibility destructive.

If it is determined that protectionism should be used to cloak non-Blacks it makes sense to include at least two groups. First, it should be available to those who are active in causes that support the African American community (e.g., education, economic, political, and health-related issues). Second, it should be used to protect non-Blacks who are connected to political issues that are important to the Black community (e.g., racial profiling, police brutality, hate crimes, and prison overcrowding). This would include those who are crime victims or community advocates. A case involving a Latino who is assaulted, beaten, or killed under circumstances comparable to those involving Abner Louima, Rodney King, or Amadou Diallo, raises issues that should concern the African American community—racial justice. The test for deciding whether to expand protectionism to members of other groups is whether a case involves an *issue* of importance to African Americans. Making Black protectionism an issue-driven practice appropriately shifts it away from the politics of personality. This change reflects the move to have critical Black protectionism address racial injustice rather than celebrity justice. This shift in focus enables Black protectionism to enhance cross-racial alliances, particularly among groups of color.

Media Affect

The media plays a central role in the operation of Black protectionism. The media's coverage of a particular story can activate or mute Black protectionism. Whether or not Black protectionism is triggered is influenced by several factors. First, the amount of media attention given to a particular case. For instance, whether there is a saturation of media coverage— how much time and space the story receives and whether it is comparable to the press attention given to other stories involving White celebrity offenders (e.g., is it a lead news story, is it widely reported). Second, the media's angle on the story. For example, when the press draws racial distinctions—e.g., between race of the victim and defendant or by surveying groups by race about the case. Third, how the press treats the person under scrutiny. Does the media stay on the story or focus on other details about the person's background (e.g., stories about the person's prior criminality, wide-ranging speculation about motivation, commentary on how the person's behavior has or will diminish the culture). Also, does the media leak private information about the case or private personal details about the person? Also, do the news stories suggest that the person is already guilty?

When one or more of the above factors is present, African American community members are more likely to rally around the fallen celebrity. When the media is perceived as piling on, or as unfairly attacking a Black celebrity, many community members focus on the media assault rather than the alleged one by the prominent African American. In this way the press, symbolically, resembles a slave master or lynch mob—determined to keep Black people, particularly those who have been successful, in their place.

Critical Black protectionism tempers the dynamic relationship between the media and Black protectionism. It imposes responsibilities on community members independent of the media's response to a particular case. Critical Black protectionism encourages African Americans to decide whether an alleged Black offender or crime victim deserves the support of the community (and if so, to determine what degree of support is appropriate). Because the revised protectionism sets in place guidelines for assessing whether protectionism is warranted, community members can avoid a media-driven response to these cases. Therefore, the decision to grant protectionism is not based on whether the media highlights or ignores a case.

In its new form, Black protectionism should cause *thinking* about whether protectionism should apply. It rejects automatic grants of protectionism. The new formulation of Black protectionism seeks to downplay the media's affect on when and how protectionism operates.

Not surprisingly, cases involving the famous, rich, and propertied command the lion's share of media time. This focus distorts the nature of anti-Black racism. Celebrities are *not* the group that is most likely to experience or be harmed by racial discrimination. Limiting Black protectionism to the famous sends a subtle message that charging Black celebrities with crime is an important and serious problem within the African American community. While crime and violence are certainly community issues, criminal charges against well-known Blacks are relatively rare. Given that most successful Blacks do not reside in Black working-class communities (where most Blacks live) celebrity incidents are far removed from the lives of the average Black person. Criminal cases involving Black celebrities represent a distant tip of the iceberg. Further, compared with the average Black person, the rich and famous are more likely to have resources to address racial affronts or injustices (e.g., ability to hire a good lawyer, access to the media). Finally, making protectionism available to the non-famous makes a clear statement that racial double standards are a problem for the entire community, not just an elite few.

All told, critical Black protectionism addresses the media's skew toward celebrities. It encourages the Black community to set its own agenda. The community decides when to speak out on behalf of a celebrity in trouble, when to rally in support of a victim of police brutality, when to acknowledge the impact of crime on Black communities, and when to publicly criticize a Black public figure for his actions.

Community Leaders

What role do African American community members have in shaping Black protectionism? First, for purposes of discussing Black protectionism, "community leaders" is broadly defined. It includes local and national level community advocates, politicians, ministers, radio and television personalities, and entertainers. It also includes the Black press (e.g., newspapers, magazines, and radio). It is fair to ask why entertainers are included within the definition of community leaders. The absence of strong national Black leadership has meant that various individuals and groups stand in the gap. It has also meant that the African Americans shape their views on race relations from a variety of sources. This section considers how Black politicians, organizations, the media, and other community leaders, can be instrumental in setting the stage for future applications of Black protectionism.

Black Political Leadership and Black Politicians

Black political leadership has an important role to play in the workings and successes of critical Black protectionism. Black politicians have a strong, long-standing base of support within the African American community. In fact, many of the early cases of Black protectionism involved politicians (see chapter 3).

Black political leadership represents a broad base of community members. It includes those who hold elective office (federal, state, or local). This group includes members of the Congressional Black Caucus and members of the local chamber of commerce. Black political leadership also includes those who are political appointees. For instance, federal or state cabinet positions, local level posts (e.g., comptroller). Political leaders are also officeholders in grassroots community organizations (e.g., the NAACP, Urban League) members of the clergy, and local community advocates. The Black church is another source of leadership within the Black community. National church-based groups, such as the National Baptist Convention, can weigh-in on particular cases (local or national) and thereby set the tone for their members. The Black church has had a long-standing role in setting the moral tone for community members. Reverends Richard Allen, Martin Luther King Jr., and Jesse Jackson are three examples.

While the tie between Black politicians and the Black community may not be as strong as it once was, politicians still play a role in setting the moral tone for the African American community—at least for some members of the community. For example, both the Congressional Black Caucus's and the NAACP's decision not to support the nomination of Clarence Thomas to the U.S. Supreme Court, sent a message to African

Americans. For instance, the NAACP's decision to revamp the nominations process after R. Kelly was nominated for an Image Award also sent a message. It was an expression of the organization's concern with how such a nomination would be perceived by the Black community and the larger public. Likewise, the fact Black political groups were largely silent in cases such as Michael Jackson and Kobe Bryant.

Therefore, whether Black politicians speak out or remain silent about a particular case, their decision sends a signal to those within the community. It also sends a message to those outside the Black community—as to what is morally acceptable, within the Black community.

In addition to Black political organizations, individual Black politicians have a role in triggering, and thus, restructuring Black protectionism. Political leaders operate at the local, state, and national level. Local and city level politicians have the potential to greatly influence community members, given that they are likely to have regular contact. Their responses to cases involving Black victims and offenders can impact community members. Therefore, if they embrace critical Black protectionism, and speak out about this, they can provide direction to community members on how to respond to particular cases.

The Black Media and Black Media Personalities

In addition to the large number of Black politicians and Black political groups, the Black media and Black media personalities have a role in shaping Black protectionism. This group includes Black-owned publications, such as *Ebony*, *Jet*, *Essence*, and various Black-owned newspapers, and websites. It can also include media that is directed at African Americans, regardless of ownership, such as BET and *Vibe* magazine. There are also a number of Black personalities who have local or national audiences. On television this includes Oprah Winfrey, Tavis Smiley, Chris Rock, and Star Jones. There are many other African Americans with high-profiles on television, however, their on-air format does not lend itself to addressing issues such as Black protectionism. For instance, the myriad television "judge" shows (e.g., Joe Brown, Mablean Ephriam, Greg Mathis, and Glenda Hatchett). Notably, each of these judges is involved in community service activities and they could use their voice beyond the bench. As judges, their knowledge of the judicial system may enhance their credibility with community members, regarding legal cases. Black radio personalities include Tom Joyner and Donnie Simpson. Joyner in particular has a national platform, which he uses regularly to address issues of social justice.

Black political organizations, politicians, local and national personalities can assist in leading the way to implement critical Black protectionism. Their voices can help to guide community responses on issues of law, ethics, and the justice system.

Should We Be Focused Elsewhere?

Critical Black protectionism is a single communal response to racial injustice. There are many others. At its best, protectionism represents a group action designed to shed light on the present-day status of race relations, through the lens of a particular case. In its ideal form, protectionism sends a loud message about how race works within the justice system and, more importantly, how race *should* work. By itself, however, protectionism can only serve as a reminder that more must be done to achieve racial equality. When it is exercised along with other community actions, protectionism can move the Black community members closer to achieving its race-related goals.

Protectionism signals the community's identification of an issue of importance for the larger group. It reflects a Black community consciousness as to how members of the community are treated and how they should be treated. Again, protectionism goes hand in hand with other strategies that seek to address racial inequality. The relationship is a dynamic one.

Is Black protectionism an important strategy in the fight for racial justice? The answer becomes apparent when another question is posed, "What would happen if the Black community did *not* engage in some form of Black protectionism?" The existence of Black protectionism offers community members a way to make a group statement. It is a practice that every community member can engage in. It is strategic, political, critical, and it reaffirms the community's commitment to racial justice. Critical Black protectionism forces reflection and analytical thought on issues that are important to the community. Adopting a critical Black protectionism approach is an indication that community members are willing to take a strong, principled stand in the fight for racial justice.

Conclusion

This chapter addresses several of the important, outstanding issues related to critical Black protectionism. First, who can apply protectionism? Specifically, whether it is appropriate to encourage people outside of the Black community to engage in the practice. Second, who can get the benefit of Black protectionism? Should it be applied to protect people outside of the African American community? A consideration of both of these questions suggests that before determining whether it can be applied by or extended beyond Blacks, it should be proven that critical Black protectionism, works. This will take some time.

In the long run, however, it makes sense that protectionism would protect anyone who works in the interests of the Black community. Those who fight for racial justice—by spreading the word that racial discrimination within the criminal justice system is *not* a thing of the past—should be encouraged to participate. This comes with a caveat. The focus of critical Black protectionism should remain squarely focused on what is in the best interests of the African American community. This focal point should not be diluted or diminished by the concerns of other racial groups. So, as long as there is agreement on the end result, all allies, from whichever racial backgrounds, should be allowed onboard.

Third, as noted, in the past, protectionism has been subject to the winds of the media. When the media is seen as coming down hard on a famous Black, community members take on a defensive pose. Critical Black protectionism, however, operates as a preemptive strike against media bias. It outlines a roadmap for action regardless of the media's response. Fourth, Black community leaders have an important role to play in encouraging community members to apply critical Black protectionism.

Finally, "protecting our own" matters because fighting for racial justice matters. Protecting our own is a testament to centuries of struggle against racism. It is a historical road sign and a contemporary warning. It represents one of the many ways that African Americans can argue that in the fight for racial justice, there is still more work to be done.

APPENDIX
Thirty-four Cases of Black Protectionism:
Potential Recipients, 1994–2004

Anthony Anderson

Actor and comedian Anthony Anderson was charged with rape in July 2004. According to the accusations, made while Anderson was on location for a movie, Anderson, along with another male actor, forced a female movie extra into a sexual encounter. Anderson denied the charges and in October 2004 a judge dismissed them as "suspicious."

Ron Artest

In December 2004, NBA player Ron Artest was charged with one count of misdemeanor assault and battery. The charges were the result of a brawl that broke out during a basketball game between the Detroit Pistons and the Indiana Pacers. After a resting Artest was doused with soda by an irate fan, Artest ran into the stands and began throwing punches at random fans. As a result of the incident, Artest was suspended for the remainder of the 2004–2005 season.

Marion Barry

In January 1990, Washington, D.C., mayor Marion Barry was captured on video smoking a crack pipe. Barry, a married man, was lured to the room by his girlfriend, Hazel Diane Moore. Moore was paid $1,700 a month to take part in the FBI sting operation. Following a jury trial, Barry was convicted of misdemeanor drug possession, acquitted on one count of drug possession, and on the remaining counts there was a hung jury. After serving a six-month federal sentence, Barry returned to Washington, D.C., and was elected mayor for a fourth term. In 2004, Barry was elected to the D.C. city council.

Bobby Brown

In 2003, entertainer Bobby Brown was charged with misdemeanor battery for striking his wife, Whitney Houston. Following an altercation, Houston called Atlanta police to her home. Brown, who has had several run-ins with the law, has served time for drunk driving; been charged with parole violations; and has been charged with probation violations for failure to make child support payments.

James Brown

In 2004, legendary soul singer James Brown was charged with criminal domestic assault. He was accused of assaulting his wife. Brown denied the charges. Over the years, Brown has had various legal scrapes. This includes a 1988 South Carolina conviction for failure to stop for a police officer, resisting arrest, gun possession, and drugs. He served a two and one-half year sentence. In 2003, the state of South Carolina granted Brown a pardon.

Kobe Bryant

In July 2003, NBA star Kobe Bryant was charged with rape. Bryant was accused of raping a nineteen-year-old White woman in his hotel room in Eagle County, Colorado. After first denying any sexual contact, Bryant later claimed the sex was consensual. Initially both Blacks and Whites expressed support for Bryant, however, the Black community showed more sympathy toward the star. In May 2004, Bryant pled not guilty to the rape charge. Following months of leaks to the press (including the publication of the victim's name and other information in sealed court documents) in September 2004, the District Attorney announced the charges against Bryant were being dismissed, because the victim refused to testify.

Bill Campbell

In August 2004, former Atlanta mayor Bill Campbell (1994–2002) was charged in a multicount federal indictment. Campbell was accused of receiving illegal campaign contributions, taking payoffs from city contractors, tax evasion, and racketeering. Campbell denied the charges, labeling them "a witch hunt."

Rae Carruth
In 1999, NFL player Rae Carruth was charged with murder. The Carolina Panthers player was accused of executing a plan to have someone shoot and kill his pregnant girlfriend, Cherica Adams. In the attack, Adams was shot in the neck. She later died and the child she was carrying was born ten weeks premature. Days following the murder, Carruth was found hiding out in the trunk of a Toyota Camry, parked in a hotel parking lot. Following a jury trial, Carruth was convicted and received a nineteen- to twenty-four-year prison sentence.

Ben Chavis
In 1994, Ben Chavis, the NAACP executive director, faced allegations of sexual harassment. His accuser, Mary Stansel, was his executive secretary. Chavis used more than $325,000 of the organization's money to settle the harassment charges. Chavis paid Stansel without consulting the NAACP's general counsel or the board of directors. After the settlement became public, it was subject to widespread criticism. In August 1994, Chavis was fired by the NAACP board. He has since become active in the Nation of Islam and has changed his name to Benjamin Chavis Muhammad.

Bill Clinton
In 1998, President Bill Clinton was accused of having sexual relations with twenty-four-year-old White House intern Monica Lewinsky. He initially denied any involvement with Lewinsky. As more evidence of their relationship surfaced, however, Clinton admitted to the extramarital affair. He was charged with perjury and obstruction of justice. Following the accusations and throughout the impeachment trial, surveys indicated that an overwhelming majority of Blacks stood behind Clinton. Clinton was impeached and ultimately acquitted in the second-ever impeachment trial in U.S. history.

Sean "Diddy" Combs
In December 1999, Sean Combs was charged with weapons possession and bribery, following a shooting in a Manhattan nightclub that left three

people injured. At the time of the incident, Combs was at the club with then-girlfriend Jennifer Lopez and an entourage of friends, including the rapper Jamal "Shyne" Barrow. After the shooting incident, a handgun was found on the floor of Combs' vehicle. Following a two-month jury trial, Combs was acquitted on all counts. Shyne was found guilty and sentenced to ten years behind bars.

Bill Cosby

In 1997, entertainer Bill Cosby admitted he had an extramarital affair with Shawn Upshaw. To keep the affair secret, Cosby paid her more than $100,000 over a twenty-year period. The affair became public after Upshaw's daughter, Autumn Jackson, attempted to extort $40 million dollars from Cosby. Jackson alleged that Cosby was her father and threatened to go public with this information unless he paid her off. Cosby has denied paternity, saying he had been only a "father figure" to Jackson. In 2005, a former Temple University employee accused Cosby of "inappropriate touching." Cosby denied the allegations and stated that his relations with the woman were consensual. No formal charges were filed by the state attorney's office.

Joycelyn Elders

Following remarks she made on World AIDS Day, U.S. Surgeon General Joycelyn Elders was harshly criticized. In 1994, Elders, in response to a question about sex education, stated that discussion of masturbation should be part of the sex education curriculum. President Clinton, who bristled at Elder's remarks, asked her to resign. He stated that Elders held views that conflicted with those of the administration.

Michael Espy

In 1994, the U.S. attorney general's office began investigating Michael Espy, the secretary of agriculture. Allegations had surfaced that Espy had unlawfully accepted gifts from individuals and organizations with business before the Department of Agriculture. There was speculation that he had received $34,000 in gifts from Tyson Foods and had acted favorably on their behalf. Following a lengthy review by the Office of the Independent Counsel, in 1997 Espy was indicted on thirty-nine counts. In 1998, following a four-year, $17 million investigation, Espy was acquitted by a federal jury.

Lani Guinier

In 1993, law professor Lani Guinier was nominated by President Bill Clinton to head the civil rights division of the U.S. attorney general's office. Guinier, a highly respected civil rights lawyer, had written widely on voting rights. Her nomination was heralded by the Left and met with extreme opposition on the Right. On the eve of her scheduled confirmation hearing, Clinton withdrew her name, stating that she had views contrary to the administration.

Alexis Herman

In 1998, Alexis Herman, secretary of labor, was accused of accepting bribes. She was investigated for allegedly receiving $250,000 in illegal campaign contributions. Following a two-year investigation, no charges were filed against Herman.

Allen Iverson

In July 2002, NBA star Allen Iverson faced criminal charges. He was accused of criminal trespass, assault, and gun possession. The charges stemmed from an incident in which Iverson was searching for his wife, who had left their home following an argument. A warrant was issued and Iverson was arrested. Later the judge dismissed twelve of the fourteen counts against Iverson—leaving two minor charges.

Janet Jackson

During the 2004 Super Bowl half-time show, Janet Jackson performed on stage with Justin Timberlake. At the end of the song, Timberlake pulled off part of Jackson's leather bustier—exposing her right breast. A loud media outcry followed the "wardrobe malfunction." Jackson, who said the routine was not supposed to reveal her bare breast, was widely accused of staging the incident as a publicity stunt. Following the incident, both Jackson and Timberlake apologized and the Federal Communications Commission fined the network. Timberlake managed to distance himself from the incident and, unlike Jackson, was allowed to attend the Grammy Awards ceremony, held later that month. Many African American celebrities questioned whether there had been a double standard in the case.

Jesse Jackson

In 2001, the Reverend Jesse Jackson, a married father of five, admitted fathering a child with his mistress, Karin Stanford. The story was widely publicized in the tabloids and the mainstream press. Jackson quickly apologized for his actions and the harms caused by them. The allegations came on the heels of Jackson's plan to lead a Florida rally to protest improprieties in the 2000 presidential election. Jackson, the head of Rainbow/PUSH and the Citizenship Education Fund, has been active in the civil rights struggle for more than forty years. The publicized affair also led to questions about $40,000 in payments Stanford received to move to Los Angeles. Throughout, polls indicated that Jackson had strong support within the African American community.

Michael Jackson

In 2003, Michael Jackson was accused of child molestation. Jackson, who faced similar charges a decade earlier, was charged with committing sexual assault against a thirteen-year-old boy. Jackson vehemently denied the allegations and stated that they were part of an extortion plot by the boy's family. Public response to the charges was mixed. Blacks, however, expressed a more favorable opinion of Jackson than Whites. In June 2005, Jackson was acquitted of all charges.

R. Kelly

In 2002, thirty-three-year-old singer R. Kelly was accused of statutory rape. Kelly, in a twenty-one-count indictment, was charged with having intercourse with a thirteen-year-old girl. The Illinois charges were based on a graphic video of the sexual encounter, which included two females, one of them a minor. When Kelly was twenty-seven, he married fifteen-year old singer Aaliyah. Throughout his career, he has faced charges of sex with minors. Kelly, known for producing music with sexually explicit lyrics, has remained a top seller. His 2002 CD,

Chocolate Factory, went double platinum and reached number one on Billboard. He was also nominated for a Grammy in 2002. Kelly's nomination for an NAACP Image award caused outrage and it was withdrawn. Many Black fans sought to distinguish between Kelly the musician and Kelly the man.

Ray Lewis

In February 2000, NFL linebacker Ray Lewis was charged with murder. The charges stemmed from a fight that broke out in front of an Atlanta nightclub. Two men were stabbed and killed. Lewis denied involvement in the deaths. In a deal with the prosecution, Lewis pled guilty to obstruction of justice and the murder charges were dropped. He was sentenced to one year of probation.

Lisa "Left Eye" Lopes

In 1994, Lisa Lopes, a member of the hip-hop group TLC, was charged with arson. Following an argument, Lopes set fire to the home she shared with her boyfriend, Atlanta Falcons player Andre Rison. The fire, which began in the bathtub, quickly engulfed the rest of the house. The home, worth more than $1 million, burned to the ground. In court, Lopes, with Rison at her side, pled guilty to first-degree arson. She was sentenced to five years probation, required to complete alcohol rehabilitation, and fined $10,000. In 2002, Lopes died in a car accident in Honduras.

Henry Lyons

The Reverend Henry Lyons was president of the National Baptist Convention. In 1997, Lyon's wife, after learning that he owned a $700,000 home with his mistress, set fire to it. The arson investigation led to a series of federal and state charges against Lyons. He was accused of bilking corporate investors out of millions of dollars. At the state level, a jury found him guilty of racketeering and grand theft. Lyons pled guilty to numerous federal charges including fraud, extortion, money laundering, and tax evasion. He was sentenced to serve five and one-half years in prison. Lyons was released from prison in 2003. He has since returned to the pulpit at a Tampa, Florida, church.

Carol Moseley-Braun

In 1992, Carol Moseley-Braun was elected to the U.S. Senate. Moseley-Braun, the first African American woman to serve in the Senate, was elected on the heels of the Clarence Thomas confirmation hearings. During her term she was accused of misusing campaign funds and criticized for maintaining an alliance with a Nigerian dictator. Moseley-Braun was never charged with criminal wrongdoing. In 1999, she was named the ambassador to New Zealand and Samoa. In 2004, Moseley-Braun was one of several candidates who sought the top spot on the Democrat's presidential ticket.

Hazel O'Leary

In 1996, Energy Secretary Hazel O'Leary began facing allegations of impropriety. O'Leary was said to have misused taxpayer's money for lavish international travel. Her trips to more than one hundred foreign countries and her domestic travel cost more than $3 million. O'Leary was also accused of making inappropriate charitable solicitations and faulted for hiring a firm to evaluate news coverage of her department. The Attorney General did not have grounds to call for an independent counsel investigation of O'Leary and no charges were filed against her. In 2004, O'Leary was named president of Fisk University.

Melvin Reynolds

In 1995, Illinois congressman Melvin Reynolds was charged with having sex with a minor. The victim, sixteen-year-old Beverly Heard, was a campaign volunteer. Reynolds, who was married, denied having any physical contact with Heard but admitted to engaging in phone sex with her. In 1997 the congressman was convicted of criminal sexual assault, child pornography, obstruction of justice, and aggravated criminal sexual abuse. Reynolds was sentenced to six and one-half years in federal prison. After serving three years, his term was commuted by President Bill Clinton.

Diana Ross

In 2002, singing legend Diana Ross was arrested in Tucson, Arizona, and charged with driving under the influence. A sobriety test indicated that

Ross's blood level was .20, more than twice the legal limit. Ross pled no contest to the charges and served a forty-eight-hour jail term. She was also sentenced to one year of unsupervised probation.

O.J. Simpson

In 1994, revered football legend O.J. Simpson was charged with murdering his wife, Nicole Brown Simpson, and her friend, Ronald Goldman. Simpson, who denied the charges, hired an all-star defense team. After an eighteen-month trial that riveted the nation, Simpson was acquitted. Simpson's court case, dubbed "the trial of the century," brought into sharp focus simmering racial tensions and divergent views on race and the justice system. Following the criminal case, Simpson was found liable in civil court for the murders and ordered to pay the Brown and Goldman families more than $30 million in compensatory and punitive damages.

Latrell Sprewell

In 1997, NBA player Latrell Sprewell was accused of choking Golden State Warriors coach P. J. Carlesimo. The videotaped incident received widespread media attention. The case came to symbolize what some believe are the excesses and problems with professional sports today. Critics have blamed the increase in athlete's salaries, the increase in high school draft picks, and the influx of African Americans into professional sports for creating a "thug-life" culture. The NBA fined and suspended Sprewell from playing for one year.

John Street

In 2003, wiretap devices were found in the office of Philadelphia's mayor, John Street. At the time the recording devices were discovered, Street was in a contentious mayoral race. The FBI, who had planted the devices, stated that Street was not the target of its surveillance. Street suggested the FBI investigation was part of a racially motivated plot—a cloaked call for the Black community's support. One week prior to the election, African American support for Street rose to 84 percent, from 70 percent. Street was reelected mayor.

Clarence Thomas

In July 1991, Clarence Thomas was nominated to fill Justice Thurgood Marshall's seat on the U.S. Supreme Court. The Black community was divided in its support of Thomas as a nominee. The African American political community was split on Thomas's nomination, some expressing support, others denouncing the choice. During a routine FBI check of Thomas, earlier allegations of sexual harassment surfaced. Anita Hill, who had been an employee of Thomas's when he was head of the EEOC, had accused him of lewd remarks and behavior. Thomas denied the allegations and claimed he was being subject to a "high-tech lynching" by the Senate Judiciary Committee. Following the allegations, there was a sharp increase in the level of Black support for Thomas. Many viewed Hill as an angry Black woman who wanted to bring down a successful Black man. In October 1991, Thomas was confirmed in a 52 to 48 Senate vote.

Mike Tyson

In 1992, prize-fighter Mike Tyson was charged with sexually assaulting an eighteen-year-old college student, Desiree Washington. Tyson met Washington at a beauty pageant. Tyson was a judge and Washington was a contestant. Tyson called Washington and they agreed to meet. Washington went to Tyson's hotel room, where according to Washington, he raped her. Tyson denied the charges. Tyson, who had been accused of earlier acts of violence, received a great deal of support from the Black community. Many believed Washington was a gold digger who made up the charges to get some of Tyson's money. Tyson was charged and convicted of rape and sentenced to serve three years in prison. Eleven years later, in 2003, Tyson stated that he would like to rape both Washington and her mother.

Jayson Williams

In 2002, Jayson Williams, a former player for the New Jersey Nets, was charged with manslaughter in the death of his chauffeur, Gus Christofi. The victim was shot when a bullet fired from a gun Williams was showing friends in the bedroom of his New Jersey mansion. Williams sought to cover up the incident by making the death look like a suicide. Williams was accused of covering up his involvement in the case. Following a four-month trial, Williams was acquitted of aggravated manslaughter and convicted of four lesser misdemeanor offenses. A mistrial was declared on the charge of reckless manslaughter.

Note

Five of these cases occurred prior to 1994: Marion Barry, Lani Guinier, Carol Moseley-Braun, Clarence Thomas, and Mike Tyson. They are included because of their importance in understanding Black protectionism.

NOTES

Chapter One

1. Throughout the book, the terms *Black* and *African American* are used interchangeably.

2. See, generally, Berkeley Art Center Association (1982), *Ethnic Notions: Black Images in the White Imagination* (text and documentary); *Black History: Lost, Stolen, or Strayed* (1968), CBS documentary; *A Century of Black Cinema* (1997), Passport Video (documentary); and the film *Bamboozled* (2000), New Line Productions. The works of Oscar Micheaux, Clarence Muse, and other pioneering Black filmmakers present a more diverse and accurate portrait of Black life.

3. "Pink-collar" refers to clerical, service, and sales positions, which are typically held by women workers.

4. In some instances these images overlap. Professional athletes and rappers embody the image of success and deviance. See generally, Todd Boyd, *Young, Black, Rich, and Famous: The Rise of the NBA, the Hip Hop Invasion, and the Transformation of American Culture* (New York: Doubleday, 2003). For further discussion of the dual nature of images of Blackness, see Katheryn K. Russell, *The Color of Crime: Racial Hoaxes, White Fear, Black Protectionism, Police Harassment, and Other Macroaggressions* (New York: New York University Press, 1998), 3–5.

5. This refers to the "onslaught of criminal images of Black men," which causes many of us to conclude, incorrectly, that Black men and crime are intrinsically linked. See Russell, *The Color of Crime*, 3.

6. See, e.g., Paul Sniderman and Thomas Piazza, *Black Pride and Black Prejudice* (Princeton, N.J.: Princeton University Press, 2002), 14–16. For instance, their findings indicate that when Blacks are asked, "How much do you think what happens to other blacks in this country will affect your life?" almost two-thirds respond "a lot," p. 15.

7. See, e.g., Sumi Cho, "Korean Americans vs. African Americans: Conflict and Construction," in Robert Gooding-Williams, ed., *Reading Rodney King, Reading Urban Uprising* (New York: Routledge, 1993).

8. See, e.g., Ellen Goodman, "Mindful of Martha," *Boston Globe*, June 30, 2002, p. H7.

9. The blue wall of silence by police is an example of group-based protectionism. See, e.g., Anthony V. Bouza, *The Police Mystique: An Insider's Look at Cops, Crime, and the Criminal Justice System* (New York: Plenum, 1990); Jerome Skolnick and David Bayley, "Potential Obstacles to Community Policing," in *Community Policing Issues and Practices around the World*, eds. Jerome Skolnick and David Bayley (Washington, D.C.: National Institute of Justice, 1988), 49–52.

10. U.S. Census Bureau (2003), "The Black Population in the United States: March 2002," p. 6 (states that 23 percent of Blacks live in poverty, compared with a rate of 12 percent for the overall population).

11. A report by the American Council on Education states that only 35 percent of the Black men who enter college graduate within six years. This is the lowest percentage of any race and gender group. The percentage for White men is 59 percent, for Hispanic men it is 46 percent, and for American Indian men it is 41 percent. The figure for Black women is 45 percent. Karen W. Arenson, "Colleges Struggle to Help Black Men Stay Enrolled," *New York Times*, December 30, 2003, p. A1. A look at the percentage of Blacks who attend college is revealing as well. Seventeen percent of Blacks who are twenty-five years and older have graduated from college, compared with 29 percent of Whites in the same age group. U.S. Census Bureau (2003), "The Black Population in the United States: March 2002," p. 2.

12. Marc Mauer and Tracy Huling, *Young Black Americans and the Criminal Justice System: Five Years Later* (Washington, D.C.: The Sentencing Project, 1995), 2. A 2002 report by the Justice Policy Institute reports that between 1999 and 2000 there were more Black men in prison or jail than there were enrolled in institutions of higher learning. Justice Policy Institute (2002), "Cellblocks or Classrooms: The Funding of Higher Education and Corrections and Its Impact on African American Men," National Summary-Fact Sheet, www.justicepolicy.org.

13. U.S. Census Bureau (2000), "Statistical Abstract of the U.S.: 2000," table 41, p. 43. The report indicates that in 1999, 45 percent of Blacks live in "owner-occupied" property. The figure for Whites is 70.3 percent.

14. The Centers for Disease Control, *National Vital Statistics Reports* 52, no. 10 (2003): 49, table 13. The study reports that 68.2 percent of Black babies are born to unmarried mothers. The figure for American Indians is 60 percent, 28.5 percent for Whites, and 15 percent for Asian/Pacific Islanders. www.cdc.gov/nchs/data/nvsr/nvsr52/nvsr52_10.pdf.

15. U.S. Census Bureau (2000), "Statistical Abstract of the U.S.: 2000," table 41, p. 43. The report indicates that in 1999, 32.5 percent of Black families were headed by a single parent. This compares with 11 percent for White families.

16. For 2002, 18 percent of all Black children were born to women under age twenty; 18.5 percent for American Indians; 10 percent for Whites; and 4 percent for Asian/Pacific Islanders (there were no separate data for Hispanics or Latinos). The Centers for Disease Control, *National Vital Statistics Reports* 52, no. 10 (2003): 49, table 13.

17. U.S. Department of Health and Human Services (2002), *TANF Annual Report to Congress*, tables 10:8, 10:22, and 10:37, p. x–207. The report indicates that between 2000 and 2001, 39 percent of those on welfare were Black. This compares with 30 percent for Whites, 26 percent for Hispanics, 2.1 percent for Asian Americans, and 1.3 percent for American Indians. www.acf.hhs.gov/programs/ofa/annualreport5/chap10.pdf.

18. U.S. Department of Education, "Drop Out Rates in the United States: 2000" (Washington, D.C.: National Center for Educational Statistics, 2000), Executive Summary, table A, p. iii. For the year 2000, 13.1 percent of all high school dropouts aged sixteen to twenty-four were Black, 7 percent White, 28 percent Hispanic, and 4 percent Asian/Pacific Islander (there were no separate figures for Hispanics or Latinos). www.nces.ed.gov/pubs2002/2002114.pdf.

19. See, e.g., figures for March 2002 that indicate that the unemployment rate for African Americans, 11 percent, was twice the rate for Whites, 5 percent. U.S. Census Bureau (2003), "The Black Population in the United States: March 2002," p. 5.

20. U.S. Census Bureau (2002), "Current Population Survey, 2002 and 2001 Annual Demographic Supplements" (Washington, D.C.: Government Accounting Office, 2002). Table 1, "Comparison of Summary Measures of Income by Selected Characteristics: 2000 and 2001."

21. U.S. Bureau of the Census (2002), *Statistical Abstract of the United States, 2002*, p. 436. See, generally, Melvin L. Oliver and Thomas M. Shapiro, *Black Wealth/White Wealth: A New Perspective on Racial Inequality* (New York: Routledge, 1995); Dalton Conley, *Being Black, Living in the Red: Race, Wealth, and Social Policy in America* (Berkeley: University of California Press, 1999).

22. Centers for Disease Control; National Center for HIV, STD, and TB Prevention, Division of HIV/AIDS Prevention (2003), Surveillance Report, Vol. 14, table 10. (The data indicate that for 2002, Blacks comprised 42 percent of persons living with AIDS. For Whites, 36 percent; and Hispanics, 20 percent.) www.cdc.gov/hiv/stats/hasr1402/table10.htm.

23. "Control rates" include prison, jail, probation, and parole. Blacks comprise 36 percent of those under the control of the criminal justice system. For Whites,

the figure is 48 percent, Hispanics, 15 percent, American Indians, under 1 percent, and Asian Americans, under 1 percent. See U.S. Department of Justice, "Prisoners in 2001" (Washington, D.C.: Government Accounting Office, 2002); U.S. Department of Justice, "Probation and Parole in the United States, 2001" (Washington, D.C.: Government Accounting Office, 2002); U.S. Department of Justice, "Prison and Jail Inmates at Midyear 2000" (Washington, D.C.: Government Accounting Office, 2001); and Katheryn Russell-Brown, *Underground Codes: Race, Crime, and Related Fires* (New York: New York University Press, 2004), 136.

24. "Illiteracy of Persons 14 Years Old and Over, By Color and Sex, By Age, Residence, and Region, for the United States: Civilian Noninstitutional Population," March 1959 (table 6).

25. Department of Commerce, Bureau of the Census; annual report, "Prisoners in State and Federal Prisons and Reformatories" (table 179).

26. Department of Commerce, Bureau of the Census (1950), "Current Population: Consumer Income, February 14, 1950," Table: Income of Families and Persons in the United States: 1948, Series P-60, no. 6; "Median Wage or Salary Income of Persons 14 Years of Age and Over with Wage or Salary Income, by Color and Major Industry Group."

27. See generally, Lawrence Friedman, *Crime and Punishment in American History* (New York: Basic, 1993); John Hope Franklin and Alfred A. Moss Jr. (1994), *From Slavery to Freedom: A History of African Americans* (New York: McGraw-Hill, 1994); and Lerone Bennett Jr., *Before the Mayflower: A History of Black America* (New York: Penguin, 1988).

28. See, e.g., *Ebony* and *Jet* magazines. Both publications chronicle Black social, political, and economic successes. *Ebony*, with 1.8 million subscribers, has the highest circulation for a Black magazine. In 2003, it ranked 38 out of 200 magazines (paid circulation in consumer magazines), www.adage.com/page (ID: AA095F).

29. See, e.g., Edwin B. Henderson, *The Negro in Sports* (Washington, D.C.: Associated Publishers, 1939), 26–30.

30. See, e.g., Arthur Ashe Jr., *A Hard Road to Glory: A History of the African-American Athlete, 1619–1918*, Vol. 1 (New York: Warner, 1988). Author quotes headlines from the July 5, 1910, *New York Times* newspaper, "Three killed in Vidalia [Georgia]. Omaha Negro Killed . . . Two Negroes Slain . . . Blacks Shoot Up Town . . . Houston Man Kills Negro," p. 38); Shirley Povich, "Nevada's Big Gamble on Boxing Has Paid Off Handsomely," *Washington Post*, February 14, 1982, p. D4 (noting an earlier *Washington Post* article that eight people had been killed in the post-fight riots); "A History of African-American Athletes," *Palm Beach Post*, February 28, 1995, p. 9D (provides timeline of sporting events,

1875–1975, involving Black athletes and notes that following the Johnson-Jeffries match there were violent riots by Whites in twelve cities).

31. Henderson, *The Negro in Sports*; Ashe Jr., *A Hard Road to Glory*, 38 (noting that city councils in Washington, D.C., Atlanta, Baltimore, St. Louis, and Cincinnati banned films of the fight).

32. *Los Angeles Times*, July 6, 1910 (editorial).

33. Chris Rock, *Roll with the New*, Dreamworks (1997).

34. Meri Nana-Ama Danquah, "Why We Really Root for O.J.: The Superstar Suspect Embodies the Illusion of a Colorblind America," *Washington Post*, July 3, 1994, p. C1.

35. This sentiment is encapsulated in a comedy routine by Richard Pryor. Pryor, after discovering that the nation's prisons are overwhelmingly populated by Black men, comments, "You go down there looking to find justice and that's what you find, 'just us.'" Richard Pryor, *Is It Something I Said?* Warner (1975).

36. Dateline NBC, Katie Couric interview with O.J. Simpson, "O.J. Simpson: 10 Years Later," June 18, 2004. http://www.msnbc.msn.com/id/5137198.

Chapter Two

1. See generally, Michael C. Dawson, *Behind the Mule: Race and Class in African-American Politics* (Princeton, N.J.: Princeton University Press, 1994).

2. See, e.g., Katheryn K. Russell, *The Color of Crime: Racial Hoaxes, White Fear, Black Protectionism, Police Harassment, and Other Macroaggressions* (New York: New York University Press, 1998), 14–25.

3. John Hope Franklin and Alfred A. Moss Jr., *From Slavery to Freedom: A History of African Americans* (New York: McGraw-Hill, 1994); Lerone Bennett Jr., *Before the Mayflower: A History of Black America* (New York: Penguin, 1988).

4. Stephen Jay Gould, *The Mismeasure of Man* (New York: Norton, 1981), 43–50.

5. Gould, *The Mismeasure of Man*, 61.

6. See Kenneth Stampp, *The Peculiar Institution: Slavery in the Ante-Bellum South* (New York: Vintage, 1956).

7. *Dred Scott v. Sandford*, 60 U.S. 393 (1857).

8. For an analysis of "racial ranking" and social science research, see Gould, *The Mismeasure of Man*. For a discussion of the effect of slavery on post-slavery society, see Glenn Loury, *The Anatomy of Racial Inequality* (Cambridge, Mass.: Harvard University Press, 2002). The author discusses "racial dishonor" as integral to the institution of slavery. Loury states, "In general, slaves are always profoundly dishonored persons. In the experience of the United States, slavery was a thoroughly racial institution. Therefore, the social meaning of race emergent in American political culture at mid-nineteenth century was closely connected with the

slaves' dishonorable status," p. 69. Loury argues that this racial dishonor is not overcome simply with the abolition of slavery:

> The *racial dishonor* of the former slaves and their descendants, historically engendered and culturally reinforced would have also to be overcome. . . . [A]n honest assessment of current American politics—its debates about welfare, crime, schools, jobs, taxes, housing, test scores, diversity, urban policy . . . reveals the lingering effects of this historically engendered dishonor. (pp. 69–70, emphasis in original)

9. *Dred Scott v. Sandford,* 60 U.S. 393 (1857).

10. Federal data report that approximately four thousand Blacks were lynched between 1882 and 1964 (the last time data were kept). U.S. Census Bureau, *Historical Statistics of the United States, Colonial Times to 1970, Bicentennial Edition, Part 2* (Washington, D.C.: Government Accounting Office, 1975), 422. Nineteenth-century lynching historian Ida B. Wells-Barnett places the figure at closer to ten thousand people. Ida B. Wells-Barnett, *On Lynchings* (Amherst, N.Y.: Humanity Books, 2002). For further discussion of the social, economic, and religious dimensions of lynchings, see generally, James Allen et al., *Without Sanctuary: Lynching Photography in America* (Santa Fe, N.Mex.: Twin Palms, 2000); Orlando Patterson, *Rituals of Blood: Consequences of Slavery in Two American Centuries* (Washington, D.C.: Civitas, 1998), 169–232; and Stewart Tolnay and E. M. Beck, *A Festival of Violence: An Analysis of Southern Lynchings, 1882–1930* (Chicago: University of Illinois Press, 1995).

11. Wells-Barnett, *On Lynchings,* 201–3.

12. Wells-Barnett, *On Lynchings,* 201–3.

13. James Allen et al., *Without Sanctuary.*

14. Patterson, *Rituals of Blood.*

15. See, e.g., Constance Curry, *Silver Rights* (Orlando, Fla.: Harcourt, 1995).

16. See, e.g., Russell, *The Color of Crime,* 19.

17. See, generally, Pauli Murray, ed., *States' Laws on Race and Color* (Athens: University of Georgia Press, 1997).

18. Douglas Massey and Nancy Denton, *American Apartheid* (Cambridge, Mass.: Harvard University Press, 1993), see pp. 36–37, 51–52, and 227–28.

19. Massey and Denton, *American Apartheid,* 74–75.

20. Massey and Denton, *American Apartheid,* 74–75.

21. Massey and Denton, *American Apartheid,* 75–78.

22. See, e.g., Eric Schmitt, "Analysis of Census Finds Segregation along with Diversity," *New York Times,* April 4, 2001.

23. Massey and Denton, *American Apartheid,* 76.

24. See, e.g., Dalton Conley, *Being Black, Living in the Red: Race, Wealth, and Social Policy in America* (Berkeley: University of California Press, 1999), 31–37.

25. Conley, *Being Black, Living in the Red*, 37. Noting that between 1930 and 1960, "fewer than 1 percent of all mortgages in the nation were issued to African Americans," citing David L. Kirp, John P. Dwyer, and Larry A. Rosenthal, *Our Town: Race, Housing, and the Soul of Suburbia* (New Brunswick, N.J.: Rutgers University Press, 1995), 7, and that the FHA "specifically prohibited lending in neighborhoods that were changing in racial or social composition."

26. The Gallup Poll reports that 85 percent of Blacks surveyed, compared with 54 percent of Whites, believe that racial profiling is a widespread practice. Further, two-thirds of Blacks, compared with one-third of Whites, stated that Blacks are treated less fairly by the police (within their own communities). The Gallup Poll (2003), "The Gallup Poll Social Audit: Black-White Relations in the United States," pp. 11–12.

27. Paul Butler describes this as "knowing what you know." Ellis Cose, ed., *The Darden Dilemma: 12 Black Writers on Justice, Race, and Conflicting Loyalties* (New York: HarperCollins, 1997), 1–19 (author refers to "those beliefs, often emotional, that are at the core of one's being and that precede or subvert education and other formal ways of knowing," p. 14).

28. See, e.g., Regina Austin, "'The Black Community,' Its Lawbreakers, and a Politics of Identification," *Southern California Law Review* 65 (1992): 1769, 1772. See also Dorothy E. Roberts, "Deviance Resistance and Love," *Utah Law Review* (1994): 179 (author observes that oppressed people "create their own concepts of justice, morality and legality," p. 180).

29. See, e.g., Derrick Bell, *Faces at the Bottom of the Well* (New York: Basic, 1992).

30. Patricia Turner, *I Heard It through the Grapevine: Rumor in African American Culture* (Berkeley: University of California Press, 1997).

31. For further discussion of the role conspiracies play within the African American community, see, e.g., Russell, *The Color of Crime*, 145–46 (discussion of conspiracies and their prevalence within African American discourse).

32. "After the Flood," radio broadcast by Ira Glass, *This American Life*, WBEZ Chicago, September 10, 2005.

33. Turner, *I Heard It through the Grapevine*, 180–201.

34. Turner, *I Heard It through the Grapevine*, 180–201.

35. Turner, *I Heard It through the Grapevine*, 180–201.

36. Regina Austin, "Beyond Black Demons & White Devils: Anti-Black Conspiracy Theorizing & the Black Public Sphere," *Florida State University Law Review* 22 (1995): 1021, 1032–33.

37. Austin, "Beyond Black Demons & White Devils," 1032–33.

38. Austin, "Beyond Black Demons & White Devils," 1032.

39. Austin, "Beyond Black Demons & White Devils," 1042.

40. Austin notes that, as a group, Blacks are particularly susceptible to believing anti-Black conspiracies. Austin, "Beyond Black Demons & White Devils," 1021.

41. Theodore Sasson, "African American Conspiracy Theories and the Social Construction of Crime," *Sociological Inquiry* 65 (1995): 265–85.

42. Sasson, "African American Conspiracy Theories," 265–85.

43. See, e.g., John Kitsuse and Malcolm Spector, "Toward a Sociology of Social Problems: Social Conditions, Value Judgments, and Social Problems," *Social Problems* 20 (1972): 407, 415.

44. In a 2003 Gallup poll, 22 percent of Blacks said as a result of race, they had been unfairly treated "in dealings with police, such as traffic incidents" in the previous month. The Gallup Poll (2003), "The Gallup Poll Social Audit: Black-White Relations in the United States," p. 12.

45. See, e.g., R. A. Lenhardt, "Understanding the Mark: Race, Stigma, and Equality in Context," *New York University Law Review* 79 (2004): 803, 806–7.

46. Trevor Gardner II, "The Political Delinquent: Crime, Deviance and Resistance in Black America," *Harvard BlackLetter Journal* 20 (2004): 141.

47. James C. Scott, *Weapons of the Weak: Everyday Forms of Peasant Resistance* (New Haven, Conn.: Yale University Press, 1985).

48. This is not surprising when we consider that a disproportionately high number of Blacks are under the control of the justice system. One in three Black men between the ages of twenty and twenty-nine are under justice system supervision. This compares with one in sixteen White men in the same age group. Thus, Blacks, compared with Whites, are more likely to know someone in the justice system. Marc Mauer and Tracy Huling, *Young Black Americans and the Criminal Justice System: Five Years Later* (Washington, D.C.: Sentencing Project, 1995), 2.

49. See, e.g., V. P. Franklin, *Black Self-Determination: A Cultural History of African-American Resistance* (Brooklyn, N.Y.: Lawrence Hill Books, 1992), 3–9. It is a historical analysis of the development of African American cultural values. The author observes, "At the core of racial consciousness that developed among Afro-Americans in the United States was the cultural objective of black self-determination, which operated in a dialectical relationship with white supremacy," p. 6.

Chapter Three

1. It is noted that in some instances, a case could be placed into more than one category. For instance, a case involving a politician accused of sexual assault (e.g., Melvin Reynolds) could be discussed under "politicians" or "sexual assault."

2. Black protectionism exists where at least one-half of the Blacks surveyed indicate that the person was innocent (or unfairly charged). Where over 50 percent of the Black community adopts a particular perspective, this indicates that the viewpoint is shared across economic lines—that Blacks who are both lower

and middle class are included. Poll data and national media reports (television and newspaper coverage) were not available for all cases.

3. See, e.g., Kevin Sack, "Pressed against a Race Ceiling." *New York Times*, April 5, 2001.

4. Joe Davidson, "Targets for Scrutiny," *Emerge Magazine*, October 1996, pp. 38–42 (quoted material, p. 40).

5. See Davidson, "Targets for Scrutiny." (Discussing charges against Harlem Congressman Adam Clayton Powell Jr. and referring to a *Washington Post* study, which found that Blacks comprised 14 percent of the 465 political corruption investigations launched from 1983 to 1988 [at a time when Blacks constituted only 3 percent of officeholders].)

6. Charles V. Hamilton, *Adam Clayton Powell Jr.: The Political Biography of an American Dilemma* (New York: Atheneum, 1991), 272.

7. Hamilton, *Adam Clayton Powell Jr.*, 270.

8. Hamilton, *Adam Clayton Powell Jr.*, 313–25.

9. Hamilton, *Adam Clayton Powell Jr.*, 13–40.

10. Hamilton, *Adam Clayton Powell Jr.*, 469.

11. Hamilton, *Adam Clayton Powell Jr.*, 478.

12. Hamilton, *Adam Clayton Powell Jr.*

13. See, e.g., Ward Churchill and Jim Vander Wall, *The COINTELPRO Papers* (Boston: South End Press, 1990).

14. Cornel West, *Race Matters* (New York: Beacon Press, 1993). Cornel West contends that there is a gaping void in Black political leadership. One result of this "crisis" (pp. 35–46) may be that the absence of leadership makes Blacks more susceptible to broad forms of racial allegiance, such as Black protectionism. The absence of principled leadership to guide community responses may make community members more susceptible to appeals to racial solidarity.

15. Tracy Thompson and Michael York, "Moore Says Barry Linked Contract, Sex: Outside Court, Mundy Calls Witness a Liar," *Washington Post*, July 4, 1990, p. A1.

16. Thompson and York, "Moore Says Barry Linked Contract, Sex."

17. Tracy Thompson and Elsa Walsh, "Jurors View Videotape of Barry Drug Arrest," *Washington Post*, June 29, 1990, p. A1.

18. Keith Harriston, "Reaction to Verdict Is Another Hung Jury; Regional Response Is Sharply Divided," *Washington Post*, August 11, 1990, p. A10.

19. Edward Walsh, "Reynolds Sentenced to 5 Years for Sex Offenses, Obstruction; Illinois Congressman Misused a 'Job for Life,' Judge Says," *Washington Post*, September 29, 1995, p. A2; Kate Grossman, "Reynolds Sprung, Thanks to Clinton; After Five Years, He's Released to Halfway House," *Chicago Sun-Times*, January 21, 2001, p. 2.

20. Walsh, "Reynolds Sentenced to 5 Years"; Grossman, "Reynolds Sprung, Thanks to Clinton."

21. Maurice Possley and Peter Kendall, "Reynolds Guilty on All Counts: Mandatory Prison Term Will Be At Least 4 Years," *Chicago Tribune*, August 23, 1995, p. 1N.

22. See Walsh, "Reynolds Sentenced to 5 Years."

23. Guy Gugliotta and John E. Yang, "Exhaustive, Damning Documents; Record Paints Conflicted Portrait," *Washington Post*, September 8, 1995, p. A1. After serving five years, Reynolds was released from prison.

24. Gugliotta and Yang, "Exhaustive, Damning Documents; Record Paints Conflicted Portrait."

25. Bill Clinton is not the only White for whom Black protectionism might be available. Rapper Eminem, who has sold millions of records, has been widely heralded and embraced by Black hip-hop fans. His racial credibility has been bolstered by the imprimatur of well-respected rapper and producer, Dr. Dre. However, Eminem's Black embrace may be less secure as a result of his negative comments about Black women. He made the statements on an early recording, which was brought to light by editors of *The Source* magazine. See, e.g., Lola Ogunnaike, "Rivals Call Emimen Racist Over Lyrics from the Past," *New York Times*, November 19, 2003, p. B3. But see Renee Graham, "After tape's release, Eminem singing new tune: I'm sorry," *San Francisco Chronicle*, December 25, 2003, p. E10 (journalist argues that the motives for releasing the tape are questionable and "It's time to move on").

26. See, e.g., Jonathan Tilove, "Black Americans Behind Clinton: President's Style Called Soulful," *Times-Picayune*, September 17, 1998. Commenting on Clinton, Rock notes, "He's the most scrutinized man in history, just as a black person would be," *Vanity Fair*, August 1998.

27. See, e.g., Debra Mathis, "The Clinton Legacy and Black America," *Savoy Magazine*, February 2001, p. 70 (article features a computer-enhanced photograph of a "Black" Bill Clinton).

28. Toni Morrison, *The New Yorker* ("Talk of the Town"), October 5, 1998, pp. 31–32.

29. Peter Baker and John F. Harris, "Clinton Admits to Lewinsky Relationship, Challenges Starr to End Personal 'Prying,'" *Washington Post*, August 18, 1998, p. A1.

30. Cecil Connolly and Robert E. Pierre, "Clinton's Strongest Constituency; To African Americans, President's Record Outweighs Personal Problems," *Washington Post*, September 17, 1998, p. A1.

31. John F. Harris, "Clinton Seeking Harlem Offices; Rent Flap Prompts a Shift Uptown," *Washington Post*, February 13, 2001, p. A1.

32. Harris, "Clinton Seeking Harlem Offices."

33. Darryl Fears, "Bill Clinton, Soul Brother? Honor Raises Some Eyebrows," *Washington Post*, October 19, 2002, p. C1.

34. George W. Grayson, "Casting D.C.'s Shadows; Statehood-Seeking 'Senators' Are as Old as the Republic," *Washington Post*, November 11, 1990, p. B5.

35. www.rainbowpush.org/pressreleases/2001/011701.htm.

36. *The National Enquirer*, January 30, 2001 (cover story).

37. Hector Tobar and Eric Slater, "Sadness, Cries of Hypocrisy Greet Jackson's Disclosure about Child Scandal: Admission about Out-of-Wedlock Baby Will Tarnish His Political, Religious Roles, Many Believe," *Los Angeles Times*, January 19, 2001, p. A1.

38. Tobar and Slater, "Sadness, Cries of Hypocrisy Greet Jackson's Disclosure about Child Scandal."

39. Tobar and Slater, "Sadness, Cries of Hypocrisy Greet Jackson's Disclosure about Child Scandal."

40. A January 24–25, 2001, Fox News/Opinion Dynamics Poll reported that 63 percent of Blacks surveyed held a favorable opinion of Jesse Jackson, compared with 24 percent of Whites.

41. Tobar and Slater, "Sadness, Cries of Hypocrisy Greet Jackson's Disclosure about Child Scandal."

42. www.abcnews.com ("Jackson Admits Affair," January 18, 2001).

43. Mike Doring, "Clinton Grants Clemency, Frees Reynolds," *Chicago Tribune*, January 21, 2001, p. 15C.

44. *Milwaukee Journal Sentinel*, "O'Hair suspect told of 'physical violence'" (wire report), January 30, 2001, p. 4A.

45. Associated Press, "Philadelphia's Mayor's Records Subpoenaed," October 19, 2003, *New York Times*, p. 30.

46. Josh Getlin, "A Bug Worsens the Fever Pitch of Politics in Philadelphia," *Los Angeles Times*, October 12, 2003, p. 20 (Street was the "subject" of the investigation).

47. See, e.g., Lynette Clemetson, "Mayor Turns U.S. Inquiry to Campaign Advantage," *New York Times*, October 31, 2003, p. A10.

48. Clemetson, "Mayor Turns U.S. Inquiry to Campaign Advantage." ("The federal authorities . . . have indicated that the listening device showed no incriminating evidence against Mr. Street.")

49. A campaign mailer sent by the Republican City Committee to voters in a conservative, mostly White neighborhood, urged them to "take back the city" from Mayor Street. Some suggested that this was a call to Whites to take back the mayor's office. Tom Barnes, "Philadelphia Mayoral Contest Offers Bugs to Hints of Scandal," *Pittsburgh Post-Gazette*, October 19, 2003, p. C-1. In response, one Democratic insider asked, "Take it back from whom? From African Americans,

obviously." At a debate between Mayor Street and Katz, one Street supporter carried a sign that read, "Ku Klux Katz." Debbie Goldberg, "Corruption Probe Roils Philadelphia Election: Racial Focus of Mayoral Clash Sharpened," *Washington Post*, October 25, 2003, p. A3.

50. It is likely that the wiretapping of Street's office was not viewed as an isolated event. Wiretapping has been used in other instances to quell Black political voices—from FBI wiretaps of Martin Luther King to the sting operation against Marion Barry. This also ties to the history of silencing the Black vote, including the 2000 presidential election in which many Black votes were not counted. At an October 2003 fund-raiser held for Mayor Street, Bill Cosby commented that the investigation was reminiscent of "what has been happening since Florida." Clemetson, "Mayor Turns U.S. Inquiry to Campaign Advantage." See also Christopher Grimes and Kamau High, "Wiretap Stirs Black Voters in Philadelphia Mayoral Poll," *Financial Times*, November 4, 2003, p. 2.

51. Goldberg, "Corruption Probe Roils Philadelphia Election."

52. Goldberg, "Corruption Probe Roils Philadelphia Election."

53. Hazel O'Leary, former energy secretary during the first Clinton administration, is not discussed separately here. Instead, the case of former labor secretary Alexis Herman, another former cabinet official, is detailed. Herman's case raises similar concerns and was treated in a similar fashion.

54. See, e.g., Monica Davey, "In Seeking Presidency, Braun Could Win Back Reputation," *New York Times*, December 18, 2003, p. A22.

55. The Federal Election Commission conducted an audit on spending for her 1992 campaign. No fines, however, were assessed against Moseley-Braun. Davey, "In Seeking Presidency, Braun Could Win Back Reputation."

56. Robert Suro, "Reno Seeks Outside Prosecutor for Herman; Allegations Involve White House Access," *Washington Post*, May 12, 1998, p. A1.

57. David A. Vise, "Labor Secretary Cleared; Influence Peddling Investigation Ends," *Washington Post*, April 6, 2000, p. A1.

58. See, e.g., Kate Hann, "Three Penn experts explore the ways politics and the press affects each other," May 26, 1994. www.upenn.edu/pennnews/current/features/1994/052694/press-forum.html.

59. Lani Guinier, "Who's Afraid of Lani Guinier?" *New York Times Magazine*, February 27, 1994, p. 40.

60. Guinier, "Who's Afraid of Lani Guinier?" (Clinton refers to Guinier's ideas as "anti-democratic" and "difficult to defend.")

61. www.surgeongeneral.gov.

62. Douglas Jehl, "Surgeon General Forced to Resign by White House," *New York Times*, December 10, 1994, p. A1.

63. Leigh Hopper, "Can't Put the Genie Back: Past Controversies Don't Daunt Joycelyn Elders Who Speaks Here Today," *Houston Chronicle*, December 1, 2000, p. A37.

64. Jehl, "Surgeon General Forced to Resign by White House."

65. For an analysis of how Black women are treated following allegations of rape and sexual assault, see Marilyn Yarbrough with Crystal Bennett, "Cassandra and the 'Sistahs': The Peculiar Treatment of African American Women in the Myth of Women as Liars," *Journal of Gender, Race, and Justice* 3 (2000): 625; Lisa Crooms, "Speaking Partial Truths and Preserving Power: Deconstructing White Supremacy, Patriarchy, and the Rape Corroboration Rule in the Interest of Black Liberation," *Howard Law Journal* 40 (1997): 459.

66. President George H. W. Bush nominated Thomas on July 1, 1991. Referring to Thomas, Bush said, "I believe he'll be a great justice. . . . The fact that he is Black and a minority has nothing to do with this in the sense that he is the best qualified at this time." John Mashek and Ethan Bronner, "Thomas a Conservative, Nominated to High Court; Confirmation Fight Expected," *Boston Globe*, July 2, 1991, p. 1.

67. Robert Chrisman and Robert Allen, eds., *The Court of Appeal: The Black Community Speaks Out on the Racial and Sexual Politics of Thomas vs. Hill* (New York: Ballantine, 1992), 269–70. On July 31, 1991, the NAACP's board of directors voted 49–1 to oppose Thomas. In a prepared statement, then-board chairman, William F. Gibson, stated:

> [T]he nomination . . . brought with it a special set of problems related to his record in several government positions—most notably as Chairman of the [EEOC], and his reactionary philosophical approach to a number of critical issues, not the least of which is affirmative action. . . . Mr. Thomas is an African-American and that fact was not ignored in our deliberations. While we feel strongly the seat should go to an African-American, we looked beyond that factor. . . . In the final analysis . . . Thomas's judicial philosophy is simply inconsistent with the historical positions taken by the NAACP. (p. 270)

The NAACP's response to Ronald Reagan's nomination of Robert Bork to the Supreme Court provides a contrast to the Thomas case. The day following the nomination, Benjamin Hooks, NAACP executive director, spoke out against Bork, stating that his nomination would "jeopardize the civil rights achievements of the past 30 years." Lou Cannon and Edward Walsh, "Reagan Nominates Appeals Judge Bork to Supreme Court; Fierce Confirmation Battle over Conservative Expected," *Washington Post*, July 2, 1987, p. A1. William T. Coleman, former NAACP board chairman, wrote an editorial for the *New York Times* opposing Bork's nomination. William T. Coleman, "Why Judge Bork Is Unacceptable,"

New York Times, September 15, 1987, p. A35. In effect, the NAACP's muted response to Thomas is an example of Black protectionism.

68. See, e.g., Richard Berke, "Black Caucus Votes to Oppose Thomas for High Court Seat," *New York Times*, July 12, 1991, p. A1 (noting that the vote was "the first official act of opposition from a Black group," that House members do not have a vote in Supreme Court confirmation hearings, and that six members abstained).

69. Chrisman and Allen, eds., *The Court of Appeal*, 286. (Reprinting statement by the Urban League, "We are hopeful that Judge Thomas's background of poverty and minority status will lead him to greater identification with those in America who today are victimized by poverty and discrimination.")

70. See, e.g., West, *Race Matters*, 27.

71. Notably, mainstream Black leadership was slow to take a public stand on the Thomas nomination. As noted, the first Black group to oppose Thomas, the Congressional Black Caucus, did not make its position known until two weeks after the nomination. It is possible that an earlier, more vigorous opposition by Black groups might have tempered Black support for Thomas.

72. Gallup poll data taken between July and October 1991 show the following race-based levels of support for Clarence Thomas's nomination to the U.S. Supreme Court:

	July-August 1991	September-October 1991*
Blacks	50%	68%
Whites	53%	52%

*Taken following disclosure of Anita Hill's allegations of sexual harassment.

See also Louis Harris, "Thomas Tacks Work: Coalition of Blacks and Conservatives, Offsets Losses among Women," *Harris Poll*, October 15, 1991: "By claiming that he was the victim of an organized effort to depict him as a stereotype of black male sexual excesses and that the hearings were directed at him because of his race, Thomas was able to increase black support for him from 58–34 to 65–32."

73. None of these theories has been established as fact in the thirteen years since the hearings. Interestingly, Thomas too was subject to a distinct, classical public framing. For an insightful analysis of how Clarence Thomas was presented to the public, see Toni Morrison, "Introduction: Friday on the Potomac," in *Raceing Justice, En-gendering Power* (New York: Pantheon, 1992), at pp. vii–xxx (discussion of how news reports and media discussions focused on Thomas's body and physicality).

74. The vote was 52 to 48. For a thorough discussion and analysis of the Thomas case see generally Morrison, "Introduction: Friday on the Potomac," and Jane Mayer and Jill Abramson, *Strange Justice: The Selling of Clarence Thomas* (Boston: Houghton Mifflin, 1994).

75. E. R. Shipp, "Final Pleas, Then Sentencing for Tyson," *New York Times,* March 26, 1992, p. B18.

76. William Gildea, "Tyson Is Released from Prison; Prays with Ali, Then Flies Home to Ohio," *Washington Post,* March 26, 1995.

77. See, e.g., Barbara Kopple's documentary *Fallen Champ: The Untold Story of Mike Tyson* (1993). One scene shows Nation of Islam leader, Minister Louis Far-rakhan, at a pro-Tyson rally. Alluding to Desiree Washington, he lectures women on the "damned deceitful games you play."

78. For a discussion of the Black community's conflicted response to Tyson, see, e.g., Clarence Page, "Hey Give Him a Break," *Baltimore Sun,* June 27, 1995, p. 11A.

79. Geoff Boucher, "Singer Kelly Arrested, Held on 21 Charges; Crime: Grand Jury Indicts R&B Star on Child Pornography Counts in Connection with Video Showing Acts with Allegedly Underage Girl," *Los Angeles Times*, June 6, 2002, p. A13.

80. In response to the charges, Kelly released the song, "Heaven I Need a Hug" (including the lyrics: "I gave 13 years of my life to this industry/ Hit song or not, I've given all of me/ You smile in my face and tell me you love me/ But then before you know the truth/ You're so quick to judge me/ Heaven I need a hug"). Jenee Osterheldt, "Does Thug Deserve a Hug? R. Kelly Fans Unsure," *Milwaukee Journal Sentinel*, July 28, 2002, p. 8B.

81. *Billboard,* "The Chart Toppers," December 27, 2003, p. 47.

82. Boucher, "Singer Kelly Arrested," p. 79.

83. Patrick O'Driscoll and Tom Kenworthy, "Whites, Blacks See Bryant Case Differently," *USA TODAY*, August 7, 2003.

84. See, e.g., Deborah Kong, "Many See Bryant Case through Race Filter," *Los Angeles Times*, August 30, 2003.

85. See, e.g., Randall Kennedy, *Race, Crime, and the Law* (New York: Pantheon, 1997), 100–104, detailing the "Scottsboro Boys" case and the related U.S. Supreme Court case, *Powell v. Alabama*, 287 U.S. 45 (1932). The 1923 racial massacre of the all-Black Rosewood, Florida, town was sparked by a false allegation that a Black man had sexually assaulted a White woman.

86. See, generally, October 2003, *Savoy Magazine* (cover story features Kobe Bryant).

87. See, e.g., "Racist Fliers in Kobe Trial Town," August 13, 2003, www.cbsnews.com/stories/2003/07; Nancy Lofholm, "Colo. Sparks Racists'

Interest Alliance: Bryant Case, Minorities Make State Fertile Ground," November 3, 2003, p. B1.

88. "Kobe T-Shirts Cause Stink in Eagle County (Sheriff does business with HangKobe.com)," November 5, 2003 (Fox news). The second style features a back that reads, "First Class Plane Ticket: $600; Hotel room; $5,000; Surgery: $25,000; Not Bringing Your Wife to Colorado With You: Priceless."

89. Jim Newton and Carla Hill, "Jackson Denies Molestation, Tells of 'Horrifying' Search," *Los Angeles Times*, December 23, 1993, p. A1.

90. "This Is Extortion: King of Pop's Brother Says Jackson Family Is 'Ready for War'" [Interview aired on ABC, November 21, 2003].

91. See, e.g., "Jackson Maintains Support of Black Fans," November 28, 2003, http://cnn.com [Jesse Jackson quoted as saying that the arrest was so "impeccably timed (it occurred the same week as the release of Jackson's new CD) that it leads to even more suspicions. It seems aimed to destroy this media mogul"]; Nekesa Mumbi Moody, "Despite Transformation, Jackson Has Black Support," *Oakland Tribune*, November 28, 2003, p. A12 (quotes several African Americans saying they support Jackson); Corey Moss, "Alicia Keys, LL Cool J, Ludacris Denounce Treatment of Jackson," November 21, 2003, www.vh1.com/news/articles/1480610/11212003/jackson_michael.jhtml. (Quoting several Black celebrities who believe Jackson was treated unfairly. Rapper LL Cool J said, "Until I see some evidence that says he's guilty, I support him publicly . . . I don't think that plastic surgery means you're a pedophile.") Some African Americans, however, have been less sympathetic. See, e.g., Aaron McGruder, "The Boondocks" (cartoon) *Oakland Tribune*, December 13, 2003, p. 9 (Living). (Panel 1: An old Black man watching television says, "Oh, here we go again with these crazy Michael Jackson allegations—LEAVE MICHAEL ALONE"; Panel 2: The old Black man continues to stare at the television set; Panel 3: Still staring at the television set, the old man says, "I mean, after you throw his crazy butt in jail, of course.")

92. USA TODAY/CNN/Gallup, December 11–14, 2003. Cesar G. Soriano, "Jackson Gets Boost in New Opinion Poll," *USA Today*, December 16, 2003.

93. A memo from the Los Angeles County Department of Children and Family Services indicated that a joint investigation with the LAPD found no proof of molestation. The investigation of the boy's relationship with Michael Jackson was conducted between February 14 and February 27, 2003. Child welfare officials said the allegations against Jackson were "unfounded." See, e.g., John M. Broder, "Jackson Is Formally Charged with Child Molesting," *New York Times*, December 19, 2003, p. A16; Charlie LeDuff, "Official Memo on Jackson Casts Doubt on Charges," *New York Times*, December 10, 2003, p. A24.

94. www.mjjsource.com.

95. Carla Marinucci and David Steele, "NBA Suspends Sprewell for a Year," *San Francisco Chronicle*, December 5, 1997, p. A1.

96. For a more detailed discussion of the relationship between gangsta rap and crime, see Katheryn Russell-Brown, *Underground Codes: Race, Crime, and Related Fires* (New York: New York University Press, 2004), 34–54.

97. Felicia R. Lee, "Cosby Defends His Remarks about Poor Blacks' Values," *New York Times*, May 22, 2004, p. A15.

98. See, e.g., Michael Eric Dyson, *Is Bill Cosby Right?: Or Has the Black Middle Class Lost Its Mind?* (New York: Civitas, 2005).

Chapter Four

1. Rob Tannenbaum, "Dave Chappelle's Wild Ride," *Blender Magazine*, August 2004, p. 114, 118–19.

2. See, e.g., Farai Chideya, "A Double Standard for War Heroes," November 14, 2003, www.alternet.org/story/17189 (accessed January 1, 2005).

3. The three focus groups, which were held in Gainesville, Florida, took place between November and December 2004. Focus groups were held at a community center and each focus group conversation was recorded and lasted between one and one-half hours. A total of thirty people participated in the focus group conversations. The discussion and analysis represents a synthesis of the three separate focus group conversations.

Chapter Five

1. www.rainbowpush.org.

2. See, e.g., Tracy Thompson and Elsa Walsh, "Jurors View Videotape of Barry Drug Arrest," *Washington Post*, June 29, 1990, p. A1.

3. Jill Nelson, "We've Been Bill-boozled," *Savoy Magazine*, May 2001, p. 46. Author labels Blacks as "the forgiving tribe" because African Americans are likely to embrace prominent community members with legal troubles.

4. E. M. Beck and Stewart Tolnay, "When Race Didn't Matter: Black and White Mob Violence against Their Own Color," in *Under Sentence of Death: Lynching in the South*, ed. W. Fitzhugh Brundage (Chapel Hill: University of North Carolina Press, 1997).

5. See, e.g., *Holder v. Hall*, 512 U.S. 874 (1994): In concurring opinion, Thomas argues that the 1965 Voting Rights Act was not intended to address racial issues such as districting and voter dilution; *Hudson v. McMillan*, 503 U.S. 1 (1992): In dissent, Thomas argues that physical abuse by prison guards is not always unconstitutional; *Adarand Constructors, Inc., v. Pena*, 515 U.S. 200 (1995): In his concurring opinion, Thomas states that affirmative action is a form of state-sanctioned

discrimination, which is always wrong, regardless of the purpose; and *Missouri v. Jenkins*, 515 U.S. 70 (1995): In a concurring opinion, Thomas argues that separate may be equal and also takes issue with the social science data used in *Brown v. Board of Education*. See, generally, Christopher Smith and Joyce A. Baugh, *The Real Clarence Thomas: Confirmation Veracity Meets Performance Reality* (New York: Lang, 2000); Stephen Wermiel, "Clarence Thomas after Ten Years: Some Reflections," *American University Journal of Gender, Social Policy & the Law* 10 (2002): 315.

6. Cornel West, *Race Matters* (New York: Beacon Press, 1993), 24.

7. West, *Race Matters*, 24.

8. West, *Race Matters*, 29.

9. Chris Rock, *Bring the Pain* video, Uni/Dreamworks, 1996.

10. Michael Eric Dyson, *Race Rules: Navigating the Color Line* (New York: Random House, 1996), 30.

11. Dyson, *Race Rules*, 30.

12. Dyson, *Race Rules*, 30.

13. Michael Jackson, "Black or White," *Dangerous* CD, Epic Records, 1991.

14. See, e.g., Katheryn K. Russell, *The Color of Crime: Racial Hoaxes, White Fear, Black Protectionism, Police Harassment, and Other Macroaggressions* (New York: New York University Press, 1998), 57–58.

15. www.bet.com.

16. DeWayne Wickham, *Bill Clinton and Black America* (New York: Ballantine, 2002), 6.

17. Wickham, *Bill Clinton and Black America*.

18. During Clinton's presidency, the incarceration rates rose to peak levels, leading some to refer to him as the "incarceration president." See Justice Policy Institute, "Too Little, Too Late: President Clinton's Legacy," www.cjcj.org/pubs/clinton/clinton.html.

19. Randall Robinson, *The Debt: What America Owes to Blacks* (New York: Dutton, 2000). Robinson elaborates:

> No segment of the national electorate has given more but demanded and received less from the Democratic Party nationally than African Americans. We [Blacks] don't take ourselves seriously, therefore no one else does. Our support can be won with gestures.

20. Wickham, *Bill Clinton and Black America*, 94 (essay by Deborah Mathis).

21. Ta-Nehisi Coates, "Soul Mates: Black America's Love Affair with Bill Clinton," *Washington Monthly*, April 2001.

22. Leonard Pitts Jr., "Being Black Isn't Enough Reason to Merit Support," *Miami Herald*, April 2, 2004.

23. National Public Radio, *The Tavis Smiley Show*, February 9, 2004.

24. Johnnetta Betsch Cole and Beverly Guy-Sheftall, *Gender Talk: The Struggle for Women's Equality in African American Communities* (New York: Ballantine, 2003), 130.

25. Betsch Cole and Guy-Sheftall, *Gender Talk*.

26. Betsch Cole and Guy-Sheftall, *Gender Talk*, 146.

27. Betsch Cole and Guy-Sheftall, *Gender Talk*, 147.

28. Michael Starr, "Star-Crossed Rosie Row," *New York Post*, May 13, 2004, www.nypost.com/entertainment/20724.htm.

29. Russell, *The Color of Crime*, 69–93.

30. This is different from playing the race card. The race card issue will persist regardless of how Black protectionism is tailored and redefined. Those who raise it will always argue that other factors are more salient than race in any particular case.

Chapter Six

1. In 2003, eighteen-year-old high school student Marcus Dixon was accused of raping a White female student. Dixon, an "A" student, was also a football standout with an athletic scholarship to Vanderbilt. Dixon maintained that the sex was consensual. There was some evidence that the young woman said she was raped because her father, an avowed racist, found out that she had slept with a Black man. Following his trial, the jury found Dixon not guilty of rape in less than thirty minutes. However, they had to convict him of violating the state's aggravated child molestation statute—which made it unlawful for someone eighteen or older to have sex with a minor. The conviction carried with it a ten-year mandatory sentence. On appeal the Georgia Supreme Court threw out the conviction. See, e.g., www.blackcommentator.com (Issue 71).

2. See e.g., "L.A. Police Officer Caught on Tape Pummeling Suspect," June 28, 2004. www.msnbc.msn.com.

3. See, e.g., U.S. Department of Justice, "Hispanic Victims of Violent Crime, 1993–2000" (Washington, D.C.: Government Accounting Office, 2002). Blacks are disproportionately more likely to be victims of violent crime than Whites. For Blacks the rate is 34.1 per 1,000 people in the population, compared with 26.5 for Whites. American Indians, however, are the racial group with the highest victimization rates—52.3 per 1,000 people in the population (p. 2).

4. See, e.g., Barbara Novovitch, "Free after 17 Years for a Rape That He Did Not Commit," *New York Times*, December 22, 2004, p. A18.

5. Katheryn K. Russell, *The Color of Crime: Racial Hoaxes, White Fear, Black Protectionism, Police Harassment, and Other Macroaggressions* (New York: New York University Press, 1998), see chapter 5 on racial hoaxes.

6. In an analysis of the role of conspiracies within the Black community, Regina Austin observes, "Although Blacks appear to be fairly quiescent and uninterested in mass political protest, there is a great deal of activity at the level of social discourse in the form of antiblack conspiracy theorizing." Regina Austin, "Beyond Black Demons and White Devils: Antiblack Conspiracy Theorizing and the Black Public Sphere," *Florida State University Law Review* 22 (1995): 1021.

7. Patricia Williams, *The Alchemy of Race and Rights: Diary of a Law Professor* (Cambridge, Mass.: Harvard University Press, 1991), 151–53, emphasis in original. In the context of analyzing "needs" versus "rights," Williams evaluates the ways that the discussion of needs has been racialized. For example, when Blacks argue that more must be done to address racial inequity, their claims are typically dismissed as self-serving. However, when Whites make the same arguments (that more must be done to ensure racial equality for Blacks), their points are more likely to be treated as unbiased statements of fact.

SELECTED BIBLIOGRAPHY

Allen, James, Hilton Als, John Lewis, and Leon Litwack, eds. *Without Sanctuary: Lynching Photography in America*. Santa Fe, N.Mex.: Twin Palms, 2000.

Ashe, Arthur Jr. *A Hard Road to Glory: A History of the African American Athlete, 1619–1918*. Vol. 1. New York: Warner, 1988.

Austin, Regina. "Beyond Black Demons and White Devils: Anti-Black Conspiracy Theorizing and the Black Public Sphere." *Florida State University Law Review* 22 (1995): 1021.

———. "'The Black Community,' Its Lawbreakers, and a Politics of Identification." *Southern California Law Review* 65 (1992): 1769.

Beck, E. M., and Stewart Tolnay. "When Race Didn't Matter: Black and White Mob Violence against Their Own Color." In *Under Sentence of Death: Lynching in the South*, ed. W. Fitzhugh Brundage. Chapel Hill: University of North Carolina Press, 1997.

Bell, Derrick. *Faces at the Bottom of the Well*. New York: Basic, 1992.

Bennett, Lerone Jr. *Before the Mayflower: A History of Black America*. East Rutherford, N.J.: Penguin, 1988.

Berkeley Art Center Association. *Ethnic Notions: Black Images in the White Imagination* (text and documentary). Berkeley, Calif., 1982.

Berlin, Ira, Marc Favreau, Robin D. G. Kelley, James H. Billington, and Steven Miller, eds. *Remembering Slavery: African Americans Talk about Their Personal Experiences of Slavery and Emancipation*. New York: New Press, 1998.

Bouza, Anthony V. *The Police Mystique: An Insider's Look at Cops, Crime, and the Criminal Justice System*. New York: Plenum, 1990.

Boyd, Todd. *Young, Black, Rich, and Famous: The Rise of the NBA, the Hip Hop Invasion, and the Transformation of American Culture*. New York: Doubleday, 2003.

Brundage, W. Fitzhugh, ed. *Under Sentence of Death: Lynching in the South.* Chapel Hill: University of North Carolina Press, 1997.

Butler, Paul. "Much Respect: Toward a Hip-Hop Theory of Punishment." *Stanford Law Review* 56 (2004): 983.

Carmichael, Stokely, and Charles V. Hamilton. *Black Power: The Politics of Liberation in America.* New York: Vintage, 1967.

The Centers for Disease Control. *National Vital Statistics Reports* 52, no. 10 (2003).

Cho, Sumi. "Korean Americans vs. African Americans: Conflict and Construction." In *Reading Rodney King, Reading Urban Uprising,* ed. Robert Gooding-Williams. New York: Routledge, 1993.

Chrisman, Robert, and Robert Allen, eds. *The Court of Appeal: The Black Community Speaks Out on the Racial and Sexual Politics of Thomas vs. Hill.* New York: Ballantine, 1992.

Churchill, Ward, and Jim Vander Wall. *The COINTELPRO Papers.* Boston: South End Press, 1990.

Coates, Ta-Nehisi. "Soul Mates: Black America's Love Affair with Bill Clinton." *Washington Monthly,* April 2001.

Cole, Johnnetta Betsch, and Beverly Guy-Sheftall. *Gender Talk: The Struggle for Women's Equality in African American Communities.* New York: Ballantine, 2003.

Conley, Dalton. *Being Black, Living in the Red: Race, Wealth, and Social Policy in America.* Berkeley: University of California Press, 1999.

Cose, Ellis, ed. *The Darden Dilemma: 12 Black Writers on Justice, Race, and Conflicting Loyalties.* New York: HarperCollins, 1997.

———. *Rage of a Privileged Class.* New York: HarperCollins, 1993.

Crenshaw, Kimberle, Neil Gotanda, Gary Peller, and Kendall Thomas, eds. *Critical Race Theory: The Key Writings That Formed the Movement.* New York: New Press, 1995.

Crooms, Lisa. "Speaking Partial Truths and Preserving Power: Deconstructing White Supremacy, Patriarchy, and the Rape Corroboration Rule in the Interest of Black Liberation." *Howard Law Journal* 40 (1997): 459.

Curry, Constance. *Silver Rights.* Orlando, Fla.: Harcourt, 1995.

Davis, F. James. *Who Is Black? One Nation's Definition.* Philadelphia: Pennsylvania State University Press, 1991.

Dawson, Michael C. *Behind the Mule: Race and Class in African American Politics.* Princeton, N.J.: Princeton University Press, 1994.

Delgado, Richard, ed. *Critical Race Theory: The Cutting Edge.* Philadelphia: Temple University Press, 1995.

Dyson, Michael Eric. *Race Rules: Navigating the Color Line*. New York: Random House, 1996.

———. *Is Bill Cosby Right?: Or Has the Black Middle Class Lost Its Mind?* New York: Civitas, 2005.

Edwards, Harry. "Why We Must Let O.J. Go: Separating Fact from Image." *Sport* 86 (1995): 80.

Feagin, Joe. *Racist America: Roots, Current Realities, and Future Reparations*. New York: Routledge, 2001.

Feagin, Joe, Hernan Vera, and Pinar Batur. *White Racism: The Basics*. New York: Routledge, 2000.

Franklin, John Hope, and Alfred A. Moss Jr. *From Slavery to Freedom: A History of African Americans*. New York: McGraw-Hill, 1994.

Franklin, V. P. *Black Self-Determination: A Cultural History of African-American Resistance*. Brooklyn, N.Y.: Lawrence Hill Books, 1992.

Friedman, Lawrence. *Crime and Punishment in American History*. New York: Basic, 1993.

Gallup Poll. "The Gallup Poll Social Audit: Black White Relations in the United States." 2003, p. 11–12.

Gardner, Trevor II. "The Political Delinquent: Crime, Deviance, and Resistance in Black America." *Harvard Blackletter Journal* 20 (2004): 141.

Garrow, David. *Bearing the Cross: Martin Luther King Jr. and the Southern Christian Leadership Conference*. New York: Morrow, 1986.

Gates, Henry Louis, and Cornel West. *The Future of the Race*. New York: Vintage, 1996.

Gladwell, Malcolm. *Blink: The Power of Thinking Without Thinking*. New York: Little, Brown, 2005.

Gould, Stephen Jay. *The Mismeasure of Man*. New York: Norton, 1981.

Grier, William H., and Price Cobbs. *Black Rage*. New York: Bantam, 1968.

Guinier, Lani. *Lift Every Voice: Turning a Civil Rights Setback into a Strong New Vision of Social Justice*. New York: Simon & Schuster, 1998.

Guinier, Lani, and Gerald Torres. *The Miner's Canary: Enlisting Race, Resisting Power, Transforming Democracy*. Cambridge, Mass.: Harvard University Press, 2003.

Hamilton, Charles V. *Adam Clayton Powell Jr.: The Political Biography of an American Dilemma*. New York: Atheneum, 1991.

Harris, David. *Profiles in Injustice: Why Racial Profiling Cannot Work*. New York: New Press, 2002.

Henderson, Edwin B. *The Negro in Sports*. Washington, D.C.: Associated Publishers, 1939.

Justice Policy Institute. "Cellblocks or Classrooms: The Funding of Higher Education and Corrections and Its Impact on African-American Men." Washington, D.C.: Justice Policy Institute, 2002. National Summary-Fact Sheet. www.justicepolicy.org.

Kennedy, Randall. *Race, Crime, and the Law.* New York: Pantheon, 1997.

Kirp, David L., John P. Dwyer, and Larry A. Rosenthal. *Our Town: Race, Housing, and the Soul of Suburbia.* New Brunswick, N.J.: Rutgers University Press, 1995.

Kitsuse, John, and Malcolm Spector. "Toward a Sociology of Social Problems: Social Conditions, Value Judgments, and Social Problems." *Social Problems* 20 (1972): 4.

Lenhardt, R. A. "Understanding the Mark: Race, Stigma, and Equality in Context." *New York University Law Review* 79 (2004): 803.

Loury, Glenn. *The Anatomy of Racial Inequality.* Cambridge, Mass.: Harvard University Press, 2002.

Markovitz, Jonathan. *Legacies of Lynching: Racial Violence and Memory.* Minneapolis: University of Minnesota Press, 2004.

Massey, Douglas, and Nancy Denton. *American Apartheid.* Cambridge, Mass.: Harvard University Press, 1993.

Mauer, Marc, and Tracy Huling. *Young Black Americans and the Criminal Justice System: Five Years Later.* Washington, D.C.: Sentencing Project, 1995.

Mayer, Jane, and Jill Abramson. *Strange Justice: The Selling of Clarence Thomas.* Boston: Houghton Mifflin, 1994.

Morrison, Toni. "The Official Story: Dead Man Golfing." In *Birth of a Nationhood: Gaze, Script, and Spectacle in the O.J. Simpson Case*, eds. Toni Morrison and Claudia Brodsky Lacour. New York: Pantheon, 1997.

———. "Introduction, Friday on the Potomac." In *Race-ing Justice, En-gendering Power*, ed. Toni Morrison. New York: Pantheon, 1992.

Murray, Pauli, ed. *States' Laws on Race and Color.* Athens: University of Georgia Press, 1997.

Oliver, Melvin L., and Thomas M. Shapiro. *Black Wealth/White Wealth: A New Perspective on Racial Inequality.* New York: Routledge, 1995.

Patterson, Orlando. *Rituals of Blood: Consequences of Slavery in Two American Centuries.* Washington, D.C.: Civitas, 1998.

Roberts, Dorothy E. "Deviance Resistance and Love." *Utah Law Review* (1994): 179.

Robinson, Randall. *The Debt: What America Owes to Blacks.* New York: Dutton, 2000.

Russell, Katheryn K. "Racial Profiling: A Status Report of the Legal, Legislative, and Empirical Literature." *Rutgers Race and the Law Review* 3 (2000): 61.

————. *The Color of Crime: Racial Hoaxes, White Fear, Black Protectionism, Police Harassment, and Other Macroaggressions.* New York: New York University Press, 1998.

Russell-Brown, Katheryn. *Underground Codes: Race, Crime, and Related Fires.* New York: New York University Press, 2004.

Sasson, Theodore. "African American Conspiracy Theories and the Social Construction of Crime." *Sociological Inquiry* 65 (1995): 265.

Scott, James C. *Weapons of the Weak: Everyday Forms of Peasant Resistance.* New Haven, Conn.: Yale University Press, 1985.

Skolnick, Jerome, and David Bayley. "Potential Obstacles to Community Policing." In *Community Policing: Issues and Practices around the World,* eds. Jerome Skolnick and David Bayley. Washington, D.C.: National Institute of Justice, 1988.

Smith, Christopher, and Joyce A. Baugh. *The Real Clarence Thomas: Confirmation Veracity Meets Performance Reality.* New York: Lang, 2000.

Sniderman, Paul, and Thomas Piazza. *Black Pride and Black Prejudice.* Princeton, N.J.: Princeton University Press, 2002.

Stampp, Kenneth. *The Peculiar Institution: Slavery in the Ante-Bellum South.* New York: Vintage, 1956.

Tolnay, Stewart, and E. M. Beck. *A Festival of Violence: An Analysis of Southern Lynchings, 1882–1930.* Chicago: University of Illinois Press, 1995.

Tucker, William H. *The Science and Politics of Racial Research.* Chicago: University of Illinois Press, 1998.

Turner, Patricia. *I Heard It through the Grapevine: Rumor in African American Culture.* Berkeley: University of California Press, 1997.

U.S. Census Bureau. "The Black Population in the United States: March 2002." Washington, D.C.: Government Accounting Office, 2003.

————. "Current Population Survey, 2002 and 2001 Annual Demographic Supplements." Washington, D.C.: Government Accounting Office, 2002.

————. *Statistical Abstract of the United States, 2002.* Washington, D.C.: Government Accounting Office, 2002.

————. *Historical Statistics of the United States, Colonial Times to 1970, Bicentennial Edition, Part 2.* Washington, D.C.: Government Accounting Office, 1975.

U.S. Department of Commerce, Bureau of the Census. Annual report, "Prisoners in State and Federal Prisons and Reformatories."

————. "Current Population: Consumer Income, February 14, 1950." 1950.

U.S. Department of Education. "Drop Out Rates in the United States: 2000." Washington, D.C.: National Center for Educational Statistics, 2000. Executive Summary, Table A, p. 111.

U.S. Department of Health and Human Services. *TANF Annual Report to Congress*. Washington, D.C.: Administration for Children and Families, 2002. Tables 10:8, 10:22, and 10:37, p. 207.

U.S. Department of Justice. "Hispanic Victims of Violent Crime, 1993–2000." Washington, D.C.: Government Accounting Office, 2002.

———. "Prisoners in 2001." Washington, D.C.: Government Accounting Office, 2002.

———. "Probation and Parole in the United States." Washington, D.C.: Government Accounting Office, 2002.

———. "Prison and Jail Inmates at Midyear 2000." Washington, D.C.: Government Accounting Office, 2001.

Wells-Barnett, Ida B. *On Lynchings*. Amherst, N.Y.: Humanity Books, 2002.

Wermiel, Stephen J. "Clarence Thomas after Ten Years: Some Reflections." *American University Journal of Gender, Social Policy & the Law* 10 (2002): 315.

West, Cornel. *Race Matters*. New York: Beacon, 1993.

Wickham, DeWayne. *Bill Clinton and Black America*. New York: Ballantine, 2002.

Williams, Patricia J. *Open House: Of Family, Friends, Food, Piano Lessons, and the Search for a Room of My Own*. New York: Farrar, Straus & Giroux, 2004.

———. *The Alchemy of Race and Rights: Diary of a Law Professor*. Cambridge, Mass.: Harvard University Press, 1991.

Yarbrough, Marilyn, and Crystal Bennett. "Cassandra and the 'Sistahs': The Peculiar Treatment of African American Women in the Myth of Women as Liars." *Journal of Gender, Race and Justice* 3 (2000): 625.

INDEX

INDEX

ABOUT THE AUTHOR

Katheryn Russell-Brown is professor of law and director of the Center for the Study of Race and Race Relations at the University of Florida, Levin College of Law. She is the author of *Underground Codes: Race, Crime, and Related Fires* (2004), and *The Color of Crime* (1998). Her 1994 article, "The Constitutionality of Jury Override in Alabama Death Penalty Cases" published in the *Alabama Law Review*, was cited in the U.S. Supreme Court's *Harris v. Alabama* (1995) decision.